Training Guide
Microsoft Access

GW00726846

Jeff Middleton

PITMAN
PUBLISHING

PITMAN PUBLISHING
128 Long Acre, London, WC2E 9AN

A Division of Longman Group UK Limited

British Library Cataloguing in Publication Data
A catologue record for this book is available from the British Library.

ISBN 0273 60417 1

Printed and bound in Singapore

Contents

Introduction

This Training Guide shows how to use the Access database while satisfying RSA, LCCI, PEI and BTEC syllabus requirements. Easy to follow tasks and discussion cover all essential features and operations necessary to become a proficient Access user. The guide can also be used for self-study.

What is a database?

A database is an organised collection of facts. The world is full of databases, for example telephone directories, railway timetables and Pizza Express menus are kinds of database.

A database is used to store, manipulate and retrieve information about people, things or events that are of interest to you.

Information and data

Database experts usually talk about data, whereas most of you think of the same kind of thing as information. There are whole books devoted to explaining the difference between the two, but the following simple explanation is sufficient.

The following is data.

Omsk	460
Tomsk	595
Gorky	420

It is quite meaningless; this is because it is raw data - data on its own without any context. If you show the same data in a meaningful context, it becomes information.

Towns in Russia	Distance from Moscow (Km)
Omsk	460
Tomsk	595
Gorky	420

This is information because you can understand what it means (even if it is of no use to you). In a database you store information, but you separate the meaning from the data as in the example above. By using a table to hold the data, you need only enter the context once - when you choose the column headings; the tables themselves contain data.

Advantages of using a database

There are many advantages of using a computerised database to store and manage your information; the following ones are the main benefits.

A great amount of information can be stored in a small space. A hard disk of the kind commonly used in a desktop computer is no larger than a paperback book, but it can often hold 100 - 400 megabytes of information. A 100 megabyte disk could hold the text from about 100 books.

A database containing valuable information can be copied onto tape or another disk, and the copy stored away from the computer. This practice - called *backing up* the information - is an insurance against a technical malfunction and other mishaps, such as fire or theft of the computer.

A database can select and present information to you in whatever order you wish. For example, in the Sunshine Holidays example database used in this book, information about holiday bookings is entered into the database as people book their holidays (so the information is entered in a fairly random order); but the database can easily produce such things as:

- an alphabetical listing, in last name order, of all the clients
- a list of people travelling on any particular holiday
- a list of people travelling on any particular date
- a list of people who have not yet paid the full amount due
- a list of bookings in invoice number order

  and so on.

This is easy to do using a computerised database, but very difficult when using non-computerised record systems where paper record cards can be kept in only one order.

A database can find a record 'card' for you when you only know a fragment of information, such as an invoice number or a person's last name (perhaps spelt incorrectly).

What is Access?

Access is a software tool that is used to build databases.

Unlike when using a word processor, which you can immediately use to produce documents, Access is first used to build a database; you can then use the database to perform the useful work of storing and retrieving your information. This database building step may only have to be done once, and is often done by an expert called a **developer**. But if your data handling needs are straightforward, Access makes it easy for you to develop your own database.

The main skill in building a database lies in understanding how a database handles the kinds of information that you wish to store, and in the design of on-screen forms and printed reports.

The main skill in using a database lies in inventing queries. A 'query' - a type of question that the database can understand - is used to extract particular information. If the query is to be used often, it can be stored in the database and re-used; it to produces an up-to-date response to the question that has been asked.

Other tasks, such as entering the data, tend to be simple and repetitive.

Access has six main components, four of which may be used by anyone, whilst Macros and Modules (not covered in this guide) are mainly intended for specialist developers who earn their living by building complex databases for other people to use.

Access Components

You can build quite sophisticated databases employing only the four 'user' components of Access.

Inside an Access database

If you could see into the 'mind' of the database, you would see that it stores data inside tables, with each column being used to record the same items of information about a different person, thing or event.

Access can quickly reorganise the data to make it appear as a set of forms (like a traditional office record card box) or on a printed report.

Unfortunately, different names are used for (almost) the same thing, depending upon whether you are discussing data as it appears in a table or on a form. This standard terminology may be confusing at first - but the following list shows the equivalent terms for referring to data when it appears in a table, and when the same data appears on a form or report.

Table view		Form view
Row	=	Record
Column	=	Field
Column name	=	Field name

Two ways of viewing your information

A table has data in columns and rows

Row
(of fields)

ROW	Title	Firstname	Lastname	Address
1	Mrs	Stella	Wanda	18 Cherry Grove
2	Mrs	Mary	Mitchell	42 Church Walk
3	Mr	Donald	Shiremoor	12 Ruskin Lane
4	Ms	Andrea	Weston	Opal Cottage
5	Mrs	Nancy	Mitchell	15 Harbour Lane
6	Mrs	Shirley	Robinson	12 Dickens Lane
7	Mr	Paul	McMullan	102 Grantham Rd
8	Ms	Samantha	Jones	195 Malting Rd
9	Mrs	Susan	Brown	11 Dickens St
10	Mr	Edward	Hart	68 Hunters Gdns
11	Mr	David	Jackson	16 St Georges St

Column
(of fields)

The same information can be presented as a set of on-screen record cards or forms

You can view any form in the stack

Fields containing data

Field names

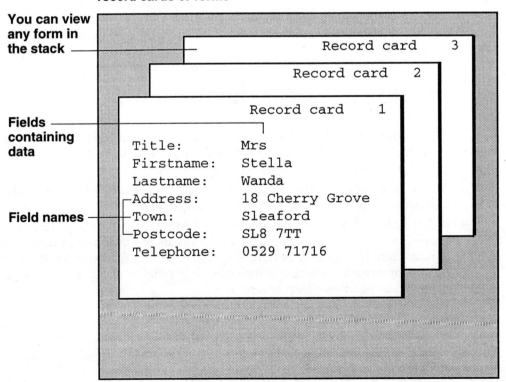

Record card   3

Record card   2

Record card   1

Title: Mrs
Firstname: Stella
Lastname: Wanda
Address: 18 Cherry Grove
Town: Sleaford
Postcode: SL8 7TT
Telephone: 0529 71716

Fields

Access can easily reorganise the data, because the way in which the tables of data are constructed makes it easy to separate individual items of data and rearrange them as required. How the data in a table appears to Access will be described in some detail because this will enable you to understand the process of building a database.

The basic building brick of a database is called a field. A database holds its data in tables, and tables are made up of fields arranged in neat rows and columns.

A field is a kind of 'box' inside the computer's memory, used to hold an item of data. The box has a name, the field name.

The field name does not mean anything to the computer - it just remembers it - so you could use names like F1, F2 or XYZ. But it is much better to use names that make it easier for humans to work with the database. Short names that tell you what kind of data is to be stored in a box are best; for example a box used to store a person's first name could sensibly be called Firstname, and one used to store a person's last name could sensibly be called Lastname.

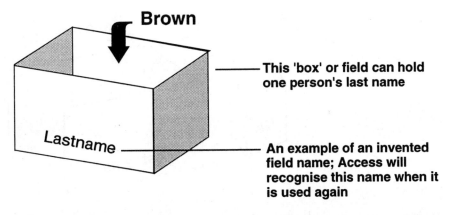

Brown

This 'box' or field can hold one person's last name

Lastname

An example of an invented field name; Access will recognise this name when it is used again

There is another aspect of field names that you need to be aware of. Because the computer does not understand the meaning of a field name - it just stores and recognises a pattern of characters - names such as Post code and Postcode appear different to Access. Conventionally, you leave out the space in field names such as Firstname, Lastname and Postcode, but Access will accept First name, Last name and Post code if you prefer these. However, once you have chosen how you are going to type a field name, you must be consistent.

Data types

You must tell Access what kind of information the box will hold, so that Access can sensibly work with the information stored in that box. For example, performing calculations with dates is not the same as calculating with numbers, and neither are the same as working with text.

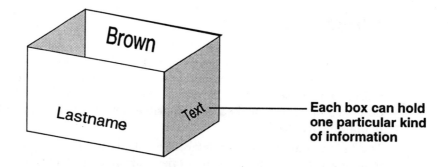

Each box can hold one particular kind of information

Field Size

Each box will have to be of a particular size. For example, a box that can hold a maximum of four characters will be smaller than one that can hold up to 20.

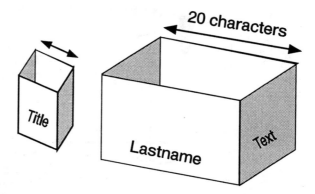

When you are designing a database you must tell Access the size of each field that you wish to use. This will be the largest size needed to contain the particular kind of information that the box will hold - for example, a Title can be Mr, Miss, Ms, Dr or Rev - the longest is four characters. So a field to hold a person's Title would be four characters wide. A Firstname or a Lastname of more than 20 characters in length is (almost) never encountered, so these fields would usually be made 20 characters wide.

When you put some data into a field, it does not matter if the field is not full.

There are two drawbacks to using fields that are larger than necessary. First, a longer field will occupy more memory, and will require more space when the database is saved (*recorded*) onto disk. Second, it will spoil the appearance of the tables, forms and reports that incorporate the oversized fields, making them inconvenient to use.

Having split up a person's full name into separate boxes, Access must have some way of connecting all the boxes that relate to one person (or thing or event that we wish to record). Access maintains links between them.

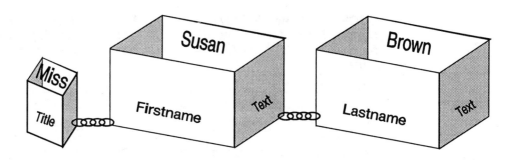

Of course, with only one of each kind of box, Access can store only one name, for example Miss Susan Brown - but once you have told Access what kind of box to use for a field, then Access can easily make any number of identical empty boxes. New boxes are made whenever new data is entered; this is how Access builds a table to hold your data.

Example database

In the course of this training guide, you will build a simple holiday booking system for a travel company called Sunshine Holidays. This example database will have two tables: one to hold customer booking details, and another to hold details about the holidays.

You store the data in two separate tables because this allows you to record the holiday details just once, instead of having to re-enter the holiday data (destination, accomodation, start date etc) with each booking. When you enter the details for each customer booking, you only enter the holiday number of the packaged tour that has been booked. When you retrieve the information, Access can take the holiday number recorded in the BOOKINGS table entry and look up the details for that holiday in the HOLIDAYS table. In this way, the Holiday Number can be used by Access to link the data in the two tables.

A relational database

This structure eliminates unnecessary duplication of data. Because Access has the ability to link the data in separate tables, using the data in related fields, Access is called a relational database. This arrangement is much more efficient than the alternative method of storing all the data in a single table.

Linking the data stored in two separate tables

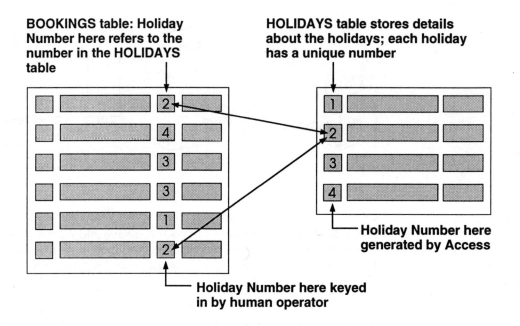

BOOKINGS table: Holiday Number here refers to the number in the HOLIDAYS table

HOLIDAYS table stores details about the holidays; each holiday has a unique number

Holiday Number here generated by Access

Holiday Number here keyed in by human operator

At least one of the two related fields must be a primary key (must contain no duplicate data entries) to ensure that, in one table, only one row is connected. In this example, the HOLIDAYS table contains the primary key used in linking the two tables.

Many databases use this structure

This way of arranging two related tables is used in many business databases. Even though the information they store is different, the database structure - the arrangement of data in separate tables which can be linked together - is often the same. For example, instead of BOOKINGS - HOLIDAYS, you could have:

STUDENTS - COURSES

EMPLOYEES - DEPARTMENTS

SALES CONTACTS - COMPANIES

PARTS - SUPPLIERS

In each case, the tables would be linked together using the data in the related fields.

Data types used in Access

When you build a database, you must tell Access what kind of information you wish to record in each field; for example, whether the information is a date, a number, currency, or text. These different kinds of information are called **data types**. The data types that can be used in Access are as follows.

Text
Used to record names, addresses and other short items of text. This is the default data type (the data type that is assumed if you do not choose a different one). Usually, the data type needed to hold any particular piece of information is fairly obvious, but sometimes you have to use a little logic - for example, a telephone number counts as text; it may contain spaces and you don't perform arithmetic upon this 'number'.

Memo
Used to store items of text where some of the entries may be quite long. The memo field is different from the other field types, having a length that increases as more text is entered into it (other types of field are of fixed length). Technically, a memo field is not part of the table (even though it appears when you view the table); the table actually holds a pointer to the memo field, which is stored elsewhere. A memo field cannot be used in as flexible a way as other fields.

Date/Time
Used to store either a date or a time (to store both you would simply use the same data type twice). Access gives you a choice of three date formats and a choice of three time formats. The format does not affect the way that the data is recorded, only the way that the data is presented to the user.

Number
This is used for numbers upon which you may wish to perform arithmetic. There are several types of number format. One special number type is the Counter field; this number automatically increments by one each time a new record is added to the table.

Currency
A number with two decimal places, suitable for US dollars and cents, British pounds and pence, or any other decimal currency. The default format uses the currency symbol for the country that has been selected in Windows.

Yes/No
This is used where the data to be entered into a field can have either of two values, such as Yes/No, On/Off etc.

OLE
Object Linking and Embedding. An OLE field can hold any type of data, including images, sounds, and video. It is often used for storing complex data - especially sounds and pictures - produced by another software application.

Using this Guide

Throughout this Guide the following terms will be used to describe operations with the mouse and keyboard:

CLICK: PRESS the left-hand mouse button briefly.

DOUBLE-CLICK: CLICK the left-hand mouse button twice in quick succession.

DRAG: PRESS and HOLD DOWN the left-hand mouse button whilst moving the mouse pointer to a new position.

SELECT: Place the mouse pointer on an item and CLICK the mouse button; the selected item becomes highlighted in some way. Normally, selecting one item de-selects any item that was previously selected, but you can hold down the Shift key whilst selecting several items.

Alternatively, to select several fields on a form or report (in Design view), DRAG the mouse over the items to enclose them in an outline; when you release the mouse button these items become selected.

CHOOSE: CLICK on a button or menu option to activate a command.

All keystroke operations are highlighted like this example: PRESS Backspace . Where variations of the phrase ENTER **Telephone** are encountered, you are required to TYPE the highlighted text and then press Enter .

Sometimes you will need to use the Shift or Ctrl key in conjunction with another key. This will be shown as, for example, Shift + F2 . This means: PRESS and HOLD DOWN the **Shift** key whilst briefly pressing the **F2** key.

Getting Started

Starting Access

To run Access, start **Windows** and DOUBLE-CLICK on the **Access icon**. If the 'Welcome to Microsoft Access' window appears, CLICK the **Close** button. After a short time, you will see the Access **Opening** window.

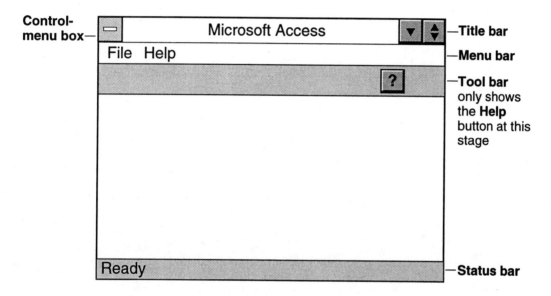

Control-menu box—

—**Title bar**

—**Menu bar**

—**Tool bar** only shows the **Help** button at this stage

—**Status bar**

Exiting Access

When in future you wish to close the Access window, CLICK on **File** to display the menu, CHOOSE **Exit**. Alternatively, you can DOUBLE-CLICK on the **Control-menu** box.

Section A
Working with tables

Task 1: To create a new database for Sunshine Holidays
Task 2: To create two tables to hold data for Bookings and Holidays
Task 3: To enter data
Task 4: To present tables on-screen in a convenient way for viewing
Task 5: To move around inside a table
Task 6: To find particular data
Task 7: To use wildcards
Task 8: To print, copy, rename and delete a table

| Task 1 | Creating a database |

➤ **This task will show you how to create a new database, how to quit Access, re-start Access, and then open the database.**

A database holds tables which hold data; the first step is to create the database itself. You must invent a name your new database; the rules for naming a database are the same as those for naming a DOS file. Briefly, a database name must:

- begin with a letter
- be no more than eight characters long
- not contain any spaces
- not use any symbols except the underline character, percent sign, minus sign, dollar, or exclamation mark.

A name should be as descriptive as possible, but because of the limited length allowed for a database name, an abbreviation of Sunshine Holidays is used.

Activity 1.1   Creating a new database, SUNHOLS

1   Start Access, CLICK on **File** to display the menu, CHOOSE **New Database**. The **New Database** window appears.

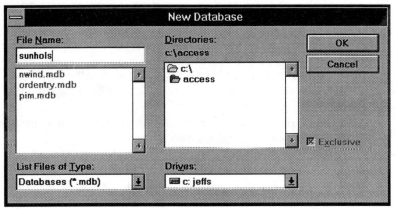

2   TYPE **sunhols**, CLICK the **OK** button. The **Database** window appears.

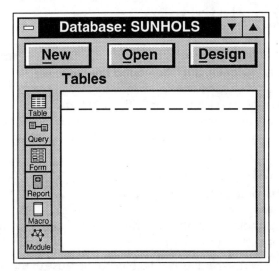

The Database window is your Access 'control center'

3   DOUBLE-CLICK on the Access window **Control-menu** box to quit Access.

Activity 1.2   Opening a database

1   DOUBLE CLICK the Access icon in the **Program Manager** window to start Access.

2   SELECT the **File** menu, CHOOSE **Open Database**. In the **Open Database** dialog we see that Access has added **.mdb** to the name (which stands for Microsoft DataBase).

3   SELECT **sunhols.mdb**, CLICK **OK**. The **Database** window appears.

Creating tables

➤ **This task will show you how to design and create tables.**

Before you begin entering data, you must create one or more 'empty' tables, each containing fields that are customised to hold the particular types of data you wish to store. A table may contain up to 255 fields. The names of fields, tables and other database objects such as queries, forms and reports should:

- begin with a letter or a number
- be no more than 64 characters long
- not use full stops, exclamation marks, or square brackets
- use any combination of letters (upper and lower case), numbers, spaces, and may use special characters such as the minus symbol or an underline.

Activity 2.1 **Creating the BOOKINGS table**

1 CLICK the **Table** button, CLICK the **New** button; the **Table** window appears.

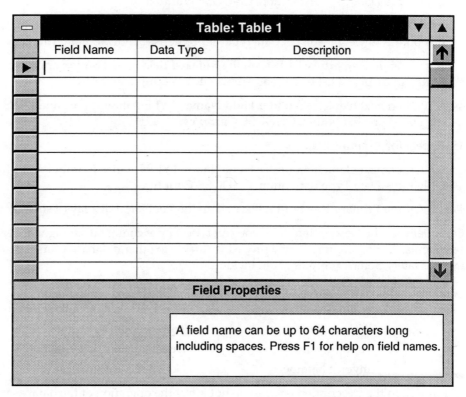

2 TYPE **Title** to name the field, PRESS Tab . The insertion point moves into the **Data Type** field, which already contains the default entry **Text**. Below, the **Field Properties** box appears.

3 CLICK on the **Field Size** field in the **Field Properties** section. PRESS $\boxed{\text{Backspace}}$ twice to delete the default entry, TYPE **4**.

4 CLICK on next blank field under **Field Name** to place the insertion point. TYPE **Firstname,** PRESS $\boxed{\text{Tab}}$. In **Field Properties**, CLICK on the **Field Size** field, PRESS $\boxed{\text{Backspace}}$ to delete the existing entry, TYPE **20**.

5 CLICK on next blank field under **Field Name**, TYPE **Lastname** and PRESS $\boxed{\text{Tab}}$.

6 In **Field Properties** set the **Field Size** to **20**. CLICK on the field labelled **Indexed**; a **list** button appears; CLICK this button to display the options, CHOOSE **Yes (Duplicates OK)**.

7 CLICK on next blank field under **Field Name**, TYPE **Address** and PRESS $\boxed{\text{Tab}}$. In **Field Properties**, set the **Field Size** to **20**.

8 CLICK on next blank **Field Name** field, TYPE **Town,** PRESS $\boxed{\text{Tab}}$. Set the **Field Size** to **20**.

9 CLICK on next blank field under **Field Name**, TYPE **Postcode** and PRESS $\boxed{\text{Tab}}$. In **Field Properties** set the **Field Size** to **8**, then CLICK on the **Format** field and TYPE a **'>'** character (to force postcodes to be upper case).

10 CLICK on next blank **Field Name** field, TYPE **Telephone** and PRESS $\boxed{\text{Tab}}$. Set the **Field Size** to **12**.

11 CLICK on next blank field under **Field Name**, TYPE **Holiday Number** and PRESS $\boxed{\text{Tab}}$. CLICK the Data Type **list** button, CHOOSE **Number**.

12 In **Field Properties**, CLICK on the **Field Size** field. A **list** button appears to the right; CLICK this button to view the list of data type sub-options, CHOOSE **Long Integer**.

13 Also in **Field Properties**, CLICK on the **Indexed** field. A **list** button appears; CLICK this button to display a list of options, CHOOSE **Yes (Duplicates OK)**.

14 CLICK on next blank field under **Field Name** , TYPE **Amount Due** and PRESS $\boxed{\text{Tab}}$. CLICK the Data Type **list** button, CHOOSE **Currency**.

15 Repeat for **Amount Paid**.

16 CLICK on next blank field under **Field Name**, TYPE **Invoice Number** and PRESS $\boxed{\text{Tab}}$. CLICK the Data Type **list** button, CHOOSE **Counter**.

17 CLICK the **Primary Key** button (located on the Toolbar, it displays a small key symbol).

Optionally, in the Description field, you can type a brief comment saying what each field name represents. A short comment may prove invaluable to other database users (or to yourself six months later). Some examples could include:

Field	Comment
Holiday Number	Number taken from the Holidays table
Amount Due	Total amount to be paid
Amount Paid	Deposit paid upon booking
Invoice Number	Generated automatically.

Comments in the Description column do not affect the operation of the database.

The table design now appears as follows.

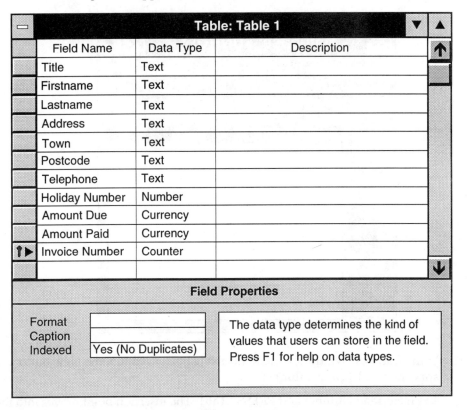

Field Name	Data Type	Description
Title	Text	
Firstname	Text	
Lastname	Text	
Address	Text	
Town	Text	
Postcode	Text	
Telephone	Text	
Holiday Number	Number	
Amount Due	Currency	
Amount Paid	Currency	
Invoice Number	Counter	

Field Properties

Format
Caption
Indexed   Yes (No Duplicates)

The data type determines the kind of values that users can store in the field. Press F1 for help on data types.

18 CLICK on **File** to display the menu, CHOOSE **Save As**. The **Save As** window appears, displaying the default name **Table1** (which we will not use).

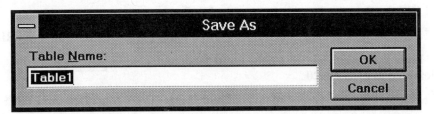

Save As

Table Name:

Table1

OK

Cancel

19 TYPE **BOOKINGS** to name your table, CLICK **OK**.

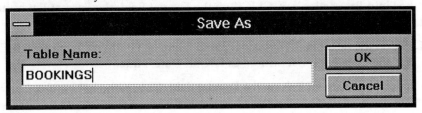

Save As

Table Name:

BOOKINGS

OK

Cancel

20 DOUBLE-CLICK the Table window **Control-menu** box (at top left of the window).

Activity 2.2   Creating the HOLIDAYS table

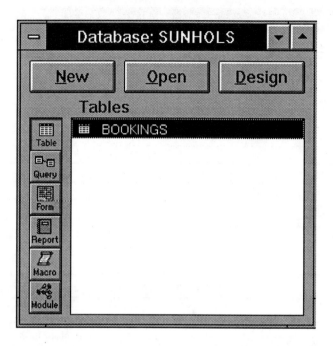

1   In the **Database** window, CLICK the **Table** button, CLICK the **New** button. A new window appears, titled **Table: Table1**.

2   TYPE **Holiday Number** and PRESS `Tab` . The insertion point moves into the next column, and the Data Type **list** button appears.

3   CLICK the **list** button to display the data types, CHOOSE **Counter**.

4   CLICK the **Primary Key** button (on the Toolbar).

5   CLICK on the next blank line under **Field Name**, TYPE **Destination** and PRESS `Tab` .

6   In **Field Properties** CLICK on the **Field Size** field, PRESS `Backspace` twice to delete the default entry, TYPE **20** .

7   CLICK on the next blank line under **Field Name**, TYPE **Start Date** and PRESS `Tab` .

8   CLICK the Data Type **list** button and CHOOSE **Date/Time**.

9   In the **Field Properties** box, CLICK on the **Format** field; the Format **list** button appears. CLICK the **list** button, CHOOSE **Medium Date**.

10 CLICK on the next blank line under **Field Name**, TYPE **Start Time** and PRESS `Tab` . CLICK the Data Type **list** button, CHOOSE **Date/Time**.

11 In **Field Properties** CLICK on the **Format** field, CLICK the **list** button, CHOOSE **Short Time**.

12 CLICK on the next blank line under **Field Name**, TYPE **Return Date** and PRESS Tab .

13 CLICK the Data Type **list** button and CHOOSE **Date/Time**.

14 In the **Field Properties** box, CLICK on the **Format** field; the Format **list** button appears. CLICK the **list** button, CHOOSE **Medium Date**.

15 CLICK on the next blank line under **Field Name**, TYPE **Return Time** and PRESS Tab . CLICK the Data Type **list** button, CHOOSE **Date/Time**.

16 In **Field Properties** CLICK on the **Format** field, CLICK the **list** button, CHOOSE **Short Time**.

17 CLICK on the next blank line under **Field Name**, TYPE **Standard Price** and PRESS Tab . CLICK the Data Type **list** button, CHOOSE **Currency**.

18 CLICK on the next blank line under **Field Name**, TYPE **Details** and PRESS Tab. CLICK the Data Type **list** button, CHOOSE **Memo**.

19 CLICK on **File** to display the menu, CHOOSE **Save As**. The **Save As** window appears. TYPE **HOLIDAYS**, CLICK **OK**. The table design appears as follows.

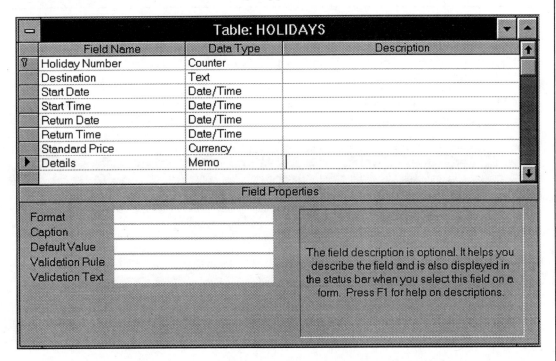

20 DOUBLE-CLICK the Table window **Control-menu** box to close this window.

21 If you wish, you may quit Access at this point. CLICK on **File**, CHOOSE **Exit** *or* alternatively DOUBLE-CLICK on the Access window **Control-menu** box.

Entering data

➤ **This task will show you how to enter the initial data for 11 bookings; a real database would have more!**

Whilst entering data, you can press either the **Tab** key or the **Enter** key to move the insertion point into the next field.

If you make a typing mistake:

- if you notice immediately, then PRESS Backspace to delete the mistake, and then re-type the data
- if you do not notice immediately, then place the mouse pointer immediately to the right of the error and CLICK to place the insertion point. Now you can PRESS Backspace to delete the mistake and re-type the data

---

Activity 3.1   **Entering data into the BOOKINGS table**

1   If necessary, start Access. CLICK on **File**, CLICK on **Open Database**, CLICK on **sunhols.mdb**, CLICK **OK**. The **Database** window appears.

2   CLICK on **BOOKINGS**, CLICK the **Open** button. The **Table** window appears with the insertion point inside the first field, ready for you to enter your data.

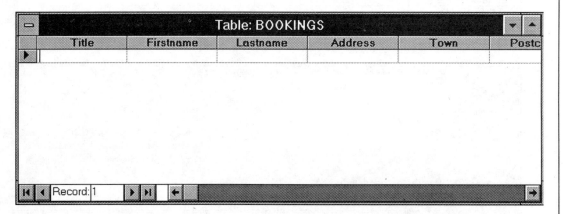

3   ENTER **Mrs.**

4   ENTER **Stella.**

5   Repeat for the other items of information in this record (do not type the commas): **Wanda, 18 Cherry Grove, Sleaford, SL8 7TT, 0529 71716, 2, 999.00, 499.00**

6   After you have entered this data, the insertion point will be in the **Invoice Number** field. Because this is a **Counter** field, Access will enter the number for you automatically. PRESS Enter to move the insertion point to the beginning of the next row.

7   ENTER the remaining records in the table.

BOOKINGS TABLE

Mrs	Stella	Wanda	18 Cherry Grove	Sleaford	SL8 7TT	0529 71716	2	999	499
Mr	David	Jackson	16 Georges St	Lincoln	LN6 8GS	0552 32189	1	135	50
Mrs	Mary	Mitchell	42 Church Walk	York	YG3 4CW	0476 2389	3	245	120
Mr	Donald	Goodman	12 Ruskin Lane	Boston	BT34 8QT	0205 33643	1	135	50
Ms	Andrea	Weston	Opal Cottage	Boston	BT5 8SC	0205 44521	1	135	50
Mrs	Nancy	Mitchell	15 Harbour Lane	Sleaford	SL3 7CL	0529 8818	3	245	100
Mrs	Shirley	Robinson	12 Dickens Lane	Melton	MN2 9DL	0664 53879	4	295	295
Mr	Paul	McMullan	102 Grant Rd	Sleaford	SL3 4GR	0529 7737	2	999	500
Ms	Sara	Jones	195 Malting Rd	Grantham	GG34 8PD	0476 5567	3	245	100
Miss	Susan	Brown	11 Dickens St	Boston	BT8 8QT	0205 98765	1	135	50
Mr	Edward	Hart	68 Hunters Lane	Redmond	WG5 2HV	0778 7734	4	295	295

The Table window looks similar to the following (only part of the table may fit onto your screen, depending upon whether you use Standard-VGA or Super-VGA).

Title	Firstname	Lastname	Address	Town	Postco
Mrs	Stella	Wanda	18 Cherry Grove	Sleaford	SL18 7TT
Mr	David	Jackson	16 Georges St	Lincoln	LN6 8GS
Mrs	Mary	Mitchell	42 Church Walk	York	YG3 4CW
Mr	Donald	Goodman	12 Ruskin Lane	Boston	BT34 8QT
Ms	Andrea	Weston	Opal Cottage	Boston	BT5 8SC
Mrs	Nancy	Mitchell	15 Harbour Lane	Sleaford	SL3 7CL
Mrs	Shirley	Robinson	12 Dickens Lane	Melton	MN2 9DL
Mr	Paul	McMullan	102 Grant Rd	Sleaford	SL3 4GR
Ms	Sara	Jones	195 Malting Rd	Grantham	GG34 8PD
Miss	Susan	Brown	11 Dickens St	Boston	BT8 8QT
Mr	Edward	Hart	68 Hunters Lane	Redmond	WG5 2HV

Table: BOOKINGS

Record: 1

8   DOUBLE-CLICK on the Table window **Control-menu** box to close the window (Access saves your data automatically).

9   If you wish, you may quit Access at this point; SELECT the **File** menu, CHOOSE **Exit**.

Optionally, when a field entry will be identical to the one above (for example, the second Boston in the table above) then you can use the 'Ditto key' to make the second entry. To enter the repeated data item, PRESS and hold down the Ctrl key whilst typing a ' (single quote).

Activity 3.2   **Entering Data into the HOLIDAYS table**

1 Start Access, SELECT the **File** menu, CHOOSE **Open Database**. From the list of databases SELECT **sunhols.mdb**, CLICK **OK**.

2 The **Database** window appears. SELECT **HOLIDAYS** then CLICK the **Open** button. The **Table** window appears.

3 PRESS $\boxed{\text{Enter}}$ to move the insertion point into the next field; because **Holiday Number** is a **Counter** field, the number will be entered for you.

4 ENTER **Le Mans/France.**

5 ENTER **17 Jun 93.**

6 ENTER **09.00.**

7 ENTER **21 Jun 93.**

8 ENTER **22.30.**

9 ENTER **150.00.**

10 TYPE the following text into the **Details** field (don't press ENTER at the end of each line).

> **Coach leaves from London Victoria. Sea crossing by ferry from Portsmouth to Le Havre in France, then by coach to Le Mans. Accommodation is in a marquee. Meals provided by cold buffet, open all day. Price includes ticket for the Le Mans 24-Hour race.**

11 PRESS $\boxed{\text{Enter}}$.

12 ENTER the following three records in the same way, by repeating steps 3 to 11.

> **Coral Sea/Australia   06 Jul 93   07.45   28 Jul 93   21.30   999.00**
>
> **By air from London Heathrow, journey includes three days in Singapore. 14 nights hotel accommodation in Cairns, on the coast near the Great Barrier Reef with its corals and endless variety of tropical fish. Scuba equipment is available for hire.**

> **Athens/Greece   08 Jul 93   14.15   16 Jul 93   07.30   245.00**
>
> **By rail from London Victoria to Gatwick airport, then by air to Athens. Eight nights hotel accommodation. Price includes several tours.**

> **St Tropez/France   18 Jul 93   14.15   26 Jul 93   22.15   295.00**
>
> **By rail from London Victoria to Gatwick airport, then by air to Toulon. Eight nights hotel accommodation. Price includes use of beach facilities and water skiing.**

13 DOUBLE-CLICK on the Table window **Control-menu** box to close the window (the new records are saved automatically).

14 If you wish, you may quit Access at this point. SELECT the **File** menu, CHOOSE **Exit**.

Viewing tables

> ➤ **This task will show you how to view, move, re-size tables, change the displayed column order and column width, open and close tables.**

You can use the Database window to display more than one table on your screen. If the Database window is obscured by the first table that you have opened, you must either move this table to the right or reduce it in size. Then you can use the Database window to open another table.

Activity 4.1   **Moving a window**

1   Start Access, SELECT the **File** menu, CHOOSE **Open Database**; the **Open Database** window appears.

2   SELECT **sunhols.mdb**, CLICK **OK**. The **Database** window appears.

3   SELECT **BOOKINGS**, CLICK the **Open** button. The **BOOKINGS** table window appears.

4   Place the mouse pointer on the **Title** bar at the top of the **Table** window. DRAG the pointer to the right. The window moves with the pointer, moving the whole table to the right. You can position the table anywhere on the screen.

Activity 4.2   **Re-sizing a window**

When positioned on the window border, the pointer appears as a double-headed arrow

Title	Firstname	Lastname	Address	Town
Mrs	Stella	Wanda	18 Cherry Grove	Sleaford
Mr	David	Jackson	16 Georges St	Lincoln
Mrs	Mary	Mitchell	42 Church Walk	York
Mr	Donald	Goodman	12 Ruskin Lane	Boston
Ms	Andrea	Weston	Opal Cottage	Boston
Mrs	Nancy	Mitchell	15 Harbour Lane	Sleaford
Mrs	Shirley	Robinson	12 Dickens Lane	Melton
Mr	Paul	McMullan	102 Grant Rd	Sleaford
Ms	Sara	Jones	195 Malting Rd	Grantham
Miss	Susan	Brown	11 Dickens St	Boston
Mr	Edward	Hart	68 Hunters Lane	Redmond

Table: BOOKINGS

Record: 4

1   Place the mouse pointer on the left-hand edge of the table window; the pointer appears as a double-headed arrow.

2   DRAG the pointer to the right. The edge of the window moves with the pointer, reducing the size of the window. You can perform this operation on any of the four sides of a window.

3   Reduce the size of the table window sufficiently to view the **Database** window underneath.

Activity 4.3   Opening a second table window

1   In the **Database** window SELECT **HOLIDAYS**, CLICK the **Open** button. The **HOLIDAYS** table window appears, overlaying any previously opened windows. You can move and re-size the window.

Activity 4.4   Viewing or editing a memo field

1   CLICK on the first row of the **Details** column in the **HOLIDAYS** table window.

2   PRESS Shift + F2 to open the **Zoom** window.

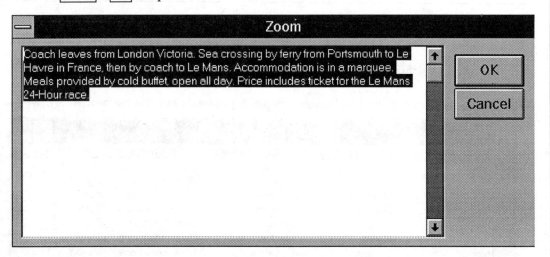

3   CLICK on the text to cancel the highlight.

4   If you wish, you may edit the text. You can use the arrow keys to move the insertion point around the text, and then PRESS the Backspace key to delete unwanted characters. Any characters that you type will be inserted into the text.

5   DOUBLE-CLICK on the Zoom window **Control-menu** box to close this window; any changes you have made are saved automatically.

Activity 4.5   **Selecting and closing a table window**

1 CLICK anywhere on the **BOOKINGS** table window (You may have to move or re-size the **HOLIDAYS** table window to do this). **BOOKINGS** becomes the currently active window, as indicated by the highlighted Title bar; the currently active window is always displayed in front of any other windows.

2 DOUBLE-CLICK on the BOOKINGS window **Control-menu** box to close this window. The **HOLIDAYS** table becomes the active window.

3 DOUBLE-CLICK on the HOLIDAYS window **Control-menu** box to close this window. The **Database** window becomes the active window.

4 If you wish, you may exit Access at this point.

Changing the column order

There are two ways of doing this. You can change the order of the fields in the Table Design window; when you display the table to view the data, you will find that the order of the columns now reflect the changes made to the table design.

Alternatively, you can move a column whilst viewing the data on-screen. If you save the file, the changes that you have made are automatically incorporated into the table design. If you do not save the file, the changes are temporary.

Activity 4.6   **Changing the column order whilst viewing the data**

1 In the **Database** window SELECT the **Table** button, SELECT **BOOKINGS**, CHOOSE **Open**.

2 CLICK on the column **selector** at the top of the **Telephone** column (the selector is the grey button at the head of a column, labelled with the column name). The column becomes highlighted.

Table: BOOKINGS

Title	Firstname	Lastname	Address	Town	Postcode	Telephone
Mrs	Stella	Wanda	18 Cherry Grove	Sleaford	SL18 7TT	0529 71716
Mr	David	Jackson	16 Georges St	Lincoln	LN6 8GS	0552 32189
Mrs	Mary	Mitchell	42 Church Walk	York	YG3 4CW	0476 2389
Mr	Donald	Goodman	12 Ruskin Lane	Boston	BT34 8QT	0205 33643
Ms	Andrea	Weston	Opal Cottage	Boston	BT5 8SC	0205 44521
Mrs	Nancy	Mitchell	15 Harbour Lane	Sleaford	SL3 7CL	0529 8818
Mrs	Shirley	Robinson	12 Dickens Lane	Melton	MN2 9DL	0664 53879
Mr	Paul	McMullan	102 Grant Rd	Sleaford	SL3 4GR	0529 7737
Ms	Sara	Jones	195 Malting Rd	Grantham	GG34 8PD	0476 5567
Miss	Susan	Brown	11 Dickens St	Boston	BT8 8QT	0205 98765
Mr	Edward	Hart	68 Hunters Lane	Redmond	WG5 2HV	0778 7734

Record: 1

3   With the pointer still on the column **selector**, DRAG the mouse pointer to the left and onto the **Address** column. When you release the mouse button the **Telephone** column is positioned to the left of the **Address** column.

Table: BOOKINGS

Title	Firstname	Lastname	Telephone	Address	Town	Postcode
Mrs	Stella	Wanda	0529 71716	18 Cherry Grove	Sleaford	SL18 7TT
Mr	David	Jackson	0552 32189	16 Georges St	Lincoln	LN6 8GS
Mrs	Mary	Mitchell	0476 2389	42 Church Walk	York	YG3 4CW
Mr	Donald	Goodman	0205 33643	12 Ruskin Lane	Boston	BT34 8QT
Ms	Andrea	Weston	0205 44521	Opal Cottage	Boston	BT5 8SC
Mrs	Nancy	Mitchell	0529 8818	15 Harbour Lane	Sleaford	SL3 7CL
Mrs	Shirley	Robinson	0664 53879	12 Dickens Lane	Melton	MN2 9DL
Mr	Paul	McMullan	0529 7737	102 Grant Rd	Sleaford	SL3 4GR
Ms	Sara	Jones	0476 5567	195 Malting Rd	Grantham	GG34 8PD
Miss	Susan	Brown	0205 98765	11 Dickens St	Boston	BT8 8QT
Mr	Edward	Hart	0778 7734	68 Hunters Lane	Redmond	WG5 2HV

Record: 1

4   CLICK anywhere else on the table to cancel the highlight; this table is more convenient for telephoning clients.

Table: BOOKINGS

Title	Firstname	Lastname	Telephone	Address	Town	Postcode
Mrs	Stella	Wanda	0529 71716	18 Cherry Grove	Sleaford	SL18 7TT
Mr	David	Jackson	0552 32189	16 Georges St	Lincoln	LN6 8GS
Mrs	Mary	Mitchell	0476 2389	42 Church Walk	York	YG3 4CW
Mr	Donald	Goodman	0205 33643	12 Ruskin Lane	Boston	BT34 8QT
Ms	Andrea	Weston	0205 44521	Opal Cottage	Boston	BT5 8SC
Mrs	Nancy	Mitchell	0529 8818	15 Harbour Lane	Sleaford	SL3 7CL
Mrs	Shirley	Robinson	0664 53879	12 Dickens Lane	Melton	MN2 9DL
Mr	Paul	McMullan	0529 7737	102 Grant Rd	Sleaford	SL3 4GR
Ms	Sara	Jones	0476 5567	195 Malting Rd	Grantham	GG34 8PD
Miss	Susan	Brown	0205 98765	11 Dickens St	Boston	BT8 8QT
Mr	Edward	Hart	0778 7734	68 Hunters Lane	Redmond	WG5 2HV

Record: 8

5   DOUBLE-CLICK on the Table window **Control-menu** box; a message appears:

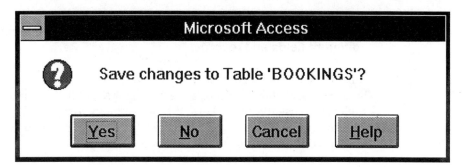

6   CHOOSE **No**. If you were to choose 'Yes' then the change that you have made to the column order is incorporated into the table design (and hence becomes permanent).

Activity 4.7   **Changing the displayed column width**

1   In the **Database** window SELECT the **Table** button, SELECT **HOLIDAYS**, CHOOSE **Open**.

2   Position the mouse pointer on the right-hand edge of a column selector; the pointer appears as a double-headed arrow passing through a vertical bar.

Starting here, drag the mouse pointer to change the column width

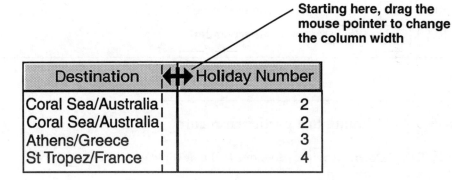

3   DRAG the mouse to the right or left to increase or decrease the width of the column.

4   Optionally, to make the changes permanent, SELECT the **File** menu, CHOOSE **Save**. Alternatively, to keep the changes temporary, close the window after viewing the table; when you are prompted to save the changes that you have made, CHOOSE **No**.

Changing the width of the column only changes the amount of data that can be displayed; it does not affect the amount of data that can be stored in the field.

Task 5 | Moving around inside a table

➤ **This task will show you how to move around inside a table, to view different fields and records.**

Whilst viewing a table, one field is highlighted (or contains the insertion point). There are many ways of moving the highlight about inside a table, of which the simplest is to use the arrow keys. When you move to a part of the table not currently displayed on screen, then the table scrolls up, down, left or right, enabling you to view a different part of the table.

Activity 5.1 **Moving to a different field**

1 From the **Database** window SELECT **BOOKINGS**, CHOOSE **Open**.

2 Check that the **Num Lock** key is **off** (Num Lock light is not illuminated).

3 PRESS the **Right arrow** key to move the highlight **one field** to the right.

4 PRESS the **Left arrow** key to move the highlight **one field** to the left.

5 PRESS **End** to move to the **last field** in the current record.

6 PRESS **Home** to move to the **first field** in the current record.

7 PRESS **Ctrl** + **PgDn** to move one **screen right**.

8 PRESS **Ctrl** + **PgUp** to move one **screen left**.

Activity 5.2 **Moving to a particular record**

1 PRESS the **Down arrow** key to move to the **next** record.

2 PRESS the **Up arrow** key to move to the **previous** record.

3 CLICK anywhere in a record to make it the **current record**. A black triangle appears at the left of the table, on the row indicator button, to indicate the current record.

Here are two commands that are especially useful when working with large tables.

4 PRESS the **Ctrl** + **Up arrow** key to move the highlight to the **first record**.

5 PRESS the **Ctrl** + **Down arrow** key to move the highlight to the **last record**.

The following instructions refer to the group of navigation buttons that appear at the lower left of the table window.

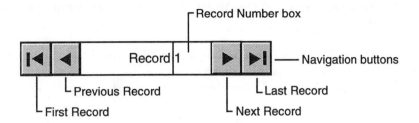

6   To move to a specific record number, CLICK on the **Record Number** box, PRESS Backspace to delete the existing entry, ENTER the **record number**.

7   PRESS F5, ENTER the **record number** as a keyboard short-cut.

8   You can also CLICK on the VCR-like navigation buttons to move between records.

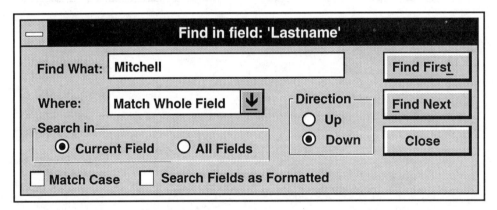

Task 6 Finding records

➤ **This task will show you how to retrieve records containing particular information.**

Access provides many ways of finding information; the simplest method is called **Find**. You can find any record provided that you know the entry in one field. Lastname is used here as an example, but you can search on any field.

Activity 6.1 **Finding a record**

1   Place the insertion point inside the **Lastname** column of the **BOOKINGS** table.

2   SELECT the **Edit** menu, CHOOSE **Find**. The **Find** window appears.

3   TYPE **Mitchell**. The **Find** window appears as follows.

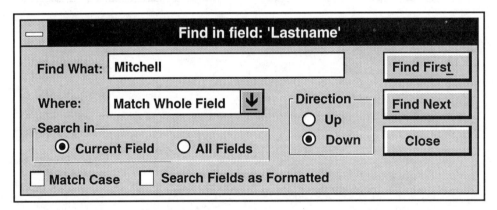

4   SELECT the **Find First** button. The first occurrence of Mitchell is highlighted (you may have to move the **Find** window to view the **BOOKINGS** table underneath).

Table: BOOKINGS

Title	Firstname	Lastname	Address	Town
Mrs	Stella	Wanda	18 Cherry Grove	Sleaford
Mr	David	Jackson	16 Georges St	Lincoln
Mrs	Mary	Mitchell	42 Church Walk	York
Mr	Donald	Goodman	12 Ruskin Lane	Boston
Ms	Andrea	Weston	Opal Cottage	Boston
Mrs	Nancy	Mitchell	15 Harbour Lane	Sleaford
Mrs	Shirley	Robinson	12 Dickens Lane	Melton
Mr	Paul	McMullan	102 Grant Rd	Sleaford
Ms	Sara	Jones	195 Malting Rd	Grantham
Miss	Susan	Brown	11 Dickens St	Boston
Mr	Edward	Hart	68 Hunters Lane	Redmond

5 CLICK the **Find Next** button to locate the next occurrence of Mitchell.

6 Repeat until all occurrences of Mitchell have been found. Access tells you when no more entries in the table meet the Find criteria. The message appears as follows.

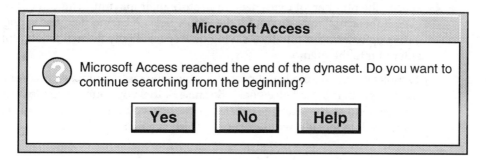

7 CLICK the **No** button. Because you used the **Find First** button you can be sure that Access started at the beginning of the table, and so all occurrences of Mitchell must have been found.

8 CLICK the Find window **Close** button to remove the window from your screen.

Searching all fields

By default, the Find command only searches the data in the current field, but you can make it search through all the fields in the table.

Memo fields behave differently from other types of field - see the next activity for how to search on a memo field.

Activity 6.2 **Searching all fields for Sleaford**

1 SELECT the **Edit** menu, CHOOSE **Find**.

2 SELECT the **All Fields** button.

3 CLICK on the **Find What** field to place the insertion point.

4 If necessary, PRESS Backspace to delete any existing entry.

5 TYPE **Sleaford.**

6 CLICK the **Find First** button; the first occurrence of Sleaford is highlighted.

7 CLICK the **Find Next** button until there is no more data that meets the find criteria.

8 CLICK the **No** button.

9 CLICK the Find window **Close** button.

10 Close the **BOOKINGS** table window.

Memo fields

Memo fields are different from the other kinds of field used in the database. 'Normal' fixed length fields always occupy the same number of bytes of storage space - the number of bytes needed to store their maximum amount of data, even if the actual data do not fill the whole field. A memo field has a length that varies up to a maximum, thus saving disk space if only a small amount of text is entered into the memo.

Technically, the memo is not part of a table - the table contains a pointer to the memo, which is stored elsewhere. Because of this you cannot use the contents of a memo field as the selection criteria in queries; you must use the Find command if you wish to locate a word or short phrase in a memo field.

Activity 6.3 **Using Find in a memo field**

1 Open the **HOLIDAYS** table and place the insertion point inside the **Details** column.

2 SELECT the **Find** button (on the Toolbar, it has a binoculars icon). The **Find** window appears.

3 TYPE **eight nights.**

4 CLICK on the Where **list** button, CHOOSE **Any Part of Field** (because the words that we are searching for may not be the first words in the field).

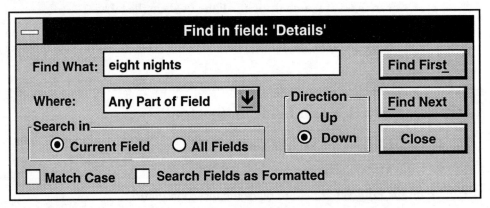

5 SELECT the **Find First** button. The first occurrence of 'eight nights' in the table is highlighted (but this part of the memo may not be visible). Close the **Find in field** window.

6 PRESS $\boxed{\text{Shift}}$ + $\boxed{\text{F2}}$ to use the **Zoom** window; when you have finished viewing the details, CLICK the **Cancel** button. CLICK the **Find** button.

7 CLICK the **Find Next** button until no more matching entries are found. A message appears; CHOOSE **No**, then CLICK the Find window **Close** button. Close the **Table** window.

Access does not understand your data, but simply recognises patterns of characters. If you had searched for the phrase '8 nights' then no match would have been found.

Using wildcards

➤ **This task will show you how to use wildcards for selecting records on the basis of inexact criteria.**

You can use a wildcard character to set selection criteria that are not exact; the wildcard characters are used to set criteria that have a certain pattern rather than exact values. There are two wildcard characters in Access; the question-mark wild card is used to replace any single character, whilst the asterisk wildcard can be used to replace any number of characters.

The question-mark wildcard is useful, for example, when you are unsure of one character in a name. Is the correct name McMullen or McMullan?

Activity 7.1 **Finding McMullan's record**

1 SELECT **BOOKINGS** in the **Database** window, CHOOSE **Open**.

2 Place the insertion point inside the **Lastname** column of the **BOOKINGS** table.

3 SELECT the **Edit** menu, CHOOSE **Find**.

4 TYPE **McMull?n**. The **Find** window appears as follows.

5 SELECT the Where **list** button, CHOOSE **Match Whole Field**.

6 CHOOSE the **Find First** button. The first (and only) occurrence of McMullan in the table is highlighted (you may have to move the **Find** window to another part of the screen to view the table).

7 CHOOSE the **Find Next** button. Access tells you that no more entries in the table meet the Find criteria; CHOOSE **No**. CHOOSE the Find window **Close** button.

The asterisk wildcard

You can use the asterisk wildcard to replace any number of characters. You can use the asterisk wildcard before a string of characters, after one or more characters (for example, "M✱" will find all clients whose Lastname begins with 'M'), or both before and after a string of characters.

This is useful when, for example, you are dealing with telephone enquiries and are unsure of the correct form of a person's name. Is the Lastname McMullan or MacMullan?

Activity 7.2 **Finding records using the asterisk wildcard**

1   Place the insertion point inside the **Lastname** column of the **BOOKINGS** table.

2   SELECT the **Edit** menu, CHOOSE **Find**.

3   TYPE **✱Mullan**.

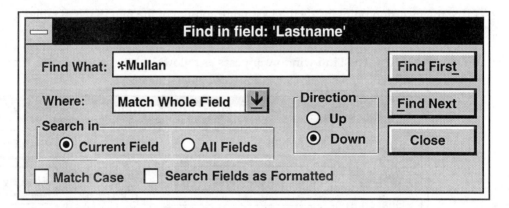

4   CHOOSE the **Find First** button. The first (and only) occurrence of McMullan in the table is highlighted.

5   CLICK the **Find Next** button. Access tells you that no more entries in the table meet the criteria. CHOOSE on **No**.

6   CHOOSE the **Find in field** window **Close** button.

7   Close the **BOOKINGS** table window.

Task 8 | Operations on a whole table

➤ **This task will show you how to print and perform other operations on a whole table.**

Activity 8.1   **Printing a table**

1 In the **Database** window, CLICK once on **BOOKINGS** to highlight the table name.

2 SELECT the **File** menu, CHOOSE **Print**.

3 When the **Print** dialog box appears, CLICK **OK** to print. When you print a table that is too large to fit onto a single page then Access will split the table and print it on multiple pages.

Copying tables

Sometimes you may wish to experiment without any danger of ruining your database. You can make a copy of a table and then safely experiment with this.

But beware! Having copies of tables is not in the spirit of using a relational database, where, as far as practical, each item of data is recorded only once. Use the copy purely for experiments, and delete it when it is no longer needed.

Activity 8.2   **Making a copy of the BOOKINGS table**

1 If necessary, CLICK on **BOOKINGS** in the **Database** window to highlight the table name.

2 SELECT the **Edit** menu, CHOOSE **Copy**.

3 SELECT **Edit**, CHOOSE **Paste**. The **Paste Table As** window appears; TYPE **BOOKINGS-2** and CHOOSE **OK**. The table appears in the **Database** window.

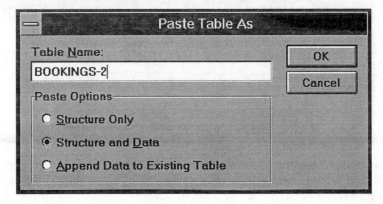

Activity 8.3   Renaming a table

1   From the **Database** window, SELECT the **Table** button, then CLICK once on **BOOKINGS-2** to highlight the table name.

2   SELECT the **File** menu, CHOOSE **Rename**; the **Rename** dialog appears.

3   TYPE **BOOKINGS-Experiments.** This is a better name because it is more descriptive.

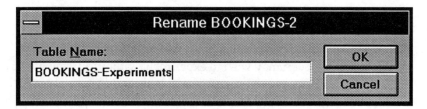

4   CHOOSE **OK** to complete.

Activity 8.4   Deleting a table

1   In the **Database** window, SELECT **BOOKINGS-Experiments**.

2   SELECT the **Edit** menu, CHOOSE **Delete**. A dialog appears, asking for confirmation. If you were to choose **OK** the table would be deleted.

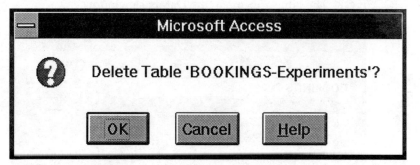

3   CHOOSE **Cancel** (because this table will be needed later). Whenever you perform a very destructive action, such as deleting a whole table, Access will give you one last chance to change your mind!

Section B
Query-by-example

| Task 9 | Creating a query

> ➤ **This task will show you how to create a query using QBE.**

Query-by-example (QBE) is a way of asking questions about the information stored in the database; it is more sophisticated than the methods you have used so far. QBE presents you with a standard Query Design window.

The Query Design window has two panes. The upper pane holds the field list for one or more tables that you have chosen to use. The lower pane contains the QBE grid, which enables you to select which fields you wish to view and specify the criteria to be used for selecting particular records. Optionally, you can perform calculations to find totals and balances etc.

When you run the query, the information extracted from the database appears in an 'answer table' that Access calls a **dynaset**. Whilst viewing a dynaset, you can change the column order or the displayed column width just as you would for a table.

A dynaset differs from a base table in two main ways. Firstly, it is a temporary thing - a new dynaset is created each time that you run the query and, secondly, it may contain data from more than one table.

A 'blank' Query Design window is shown below. It looks complicated at first sight, but it is very easy to use.

Field list

QBE grid

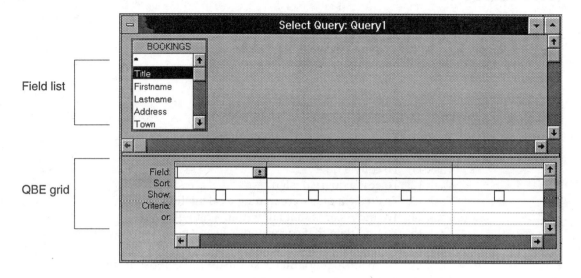

Activity 9.1   **Producing a list of clients booked on Holiday 3**

1   From the **Database** window SELECT the **Query** button, CHOOSE **New**. This puts Access into *Query Design mode*. The **Select Query** window appears with the **Add Table** dialog box superimposed.

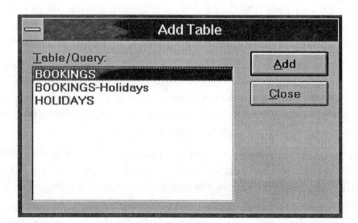

2   SELECT **BOOKINGS** (if it is not already selected) then CHOOSE **Add**.

3   Close the **Add Table** window.

The BOOKINGS field list appears towards the upper left of the Select Query window; you can ignore this for now. The following instructions refer to the QBE grid that appears in the lower pane of the window.

4 CLICK the **list** button that appears at the top right of the first column; a list of field names from the **BOOKINGS** table appears. CHOOSE **Title**.

5 CLICK at the top of the second column, SELECT the **list** button, CHOOSE **Firstname.**

From now on you will use a quicker method of placing the field names into the query definition, which you can use when a field name is to be placed into the next unused column.

6 DOUBLE-CLICK on **Lastname** in the **BOOKINGS** field list; the **Lastname** field appears in the QBE grid.

7 Use the **scroll-bar** in the **BOOKINGS** field list to bring **Holiday Number** into view. DOUBLE-CLICK on **Holiday Number**; the field appears in the QBE grid.

8 DOUBLE-CLICK on **Telephone**; the field appears in the QBE grid.

You may wish to use a criteria field to select particular records, otherwise all records are selected. Here you will select those clients who have booked Holiday Number 3.

9 CLICK on the **Criteria** field in the **Holiday Number** column in the QBE grid, TYPE **3**.

10 CLICK on the **Show** check box (to clear it, so that the **Holiday Number** data will not appear in the dynaset).

Optionally, the result of making the query can be sorted in order using the data in any field; you will use Lastname.

11 CLICK on the **Sort** row of the **Lastname** column. CLICK the **list** button, CHOOSE **Ascending**. The **Query Design** window appears as follows.

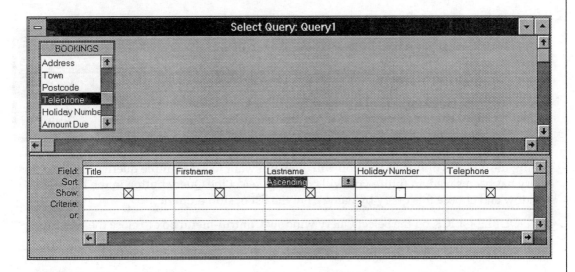

12 SELECT the **Query** menu, CHOOSE **Run**. The dynaset appears, displaying the data that you have selected from the **BOOKINGS** table.

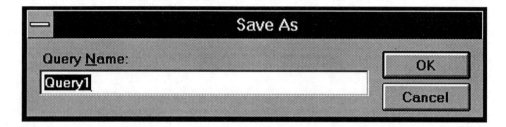

13 SELECT the **File** menu, CHOOSE **Save Query As.**

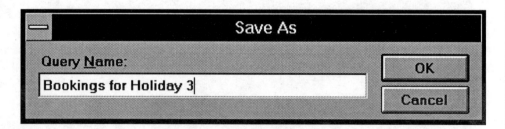

14 ENTER a brief descriptive name such as **Bookings for Holiday 3** then CHOOSE **OK**. This saves the query definition, not the dynaset produced by running the query.

Save As

Query Name:

Bookings for Holiday 3

OK

Cancel

Saving the query is optional, and you will often not want to save simple queries. Because this query has been saved, in future you will be able to select the Query button in the Database window and choose this query by name from the list of stored queries.

15 DOUBLE-CLICK on the Select Query window **Control-menu** box to close the window.

Activity 9.2   Re-using a stored query

From the Database window you can retrieve a stored query; it is automatically run for you.

1   SELECT the **Query** button in the **Database** window; a list of stored queries is displayed.

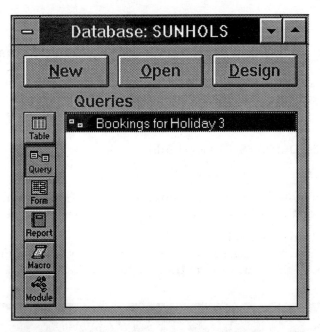

2   SELECT **Bookings for Holiday 3** (if this is the only query as yet stored, then it will already be selected).

3   CHOOSE the **Open** button; the following dynaset is produced.

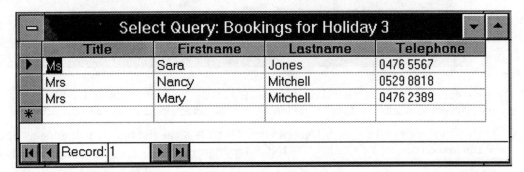

	Title	Firstname	Lastname	Telephone
▶	Ms	Sara	Jones	0476 5567
	Mrs	Nancy	Mitchell	0529 8818
	Mrs	Mary	Mitchell	0476 2389
*				

When a stored query is re-used it will produce a new dynaset that reflects any changes that may have been made to the data in the table.

Task 10 Queries using data from two tables

➤ **This task will show you how to design a query to extract data from two tables which have been linked together.**

Activity 10.1 **Making a telephone list showing destinations**

1 From the **Database** window SELECT **Query**, CHOOSE **New**. The **Query Design** window appears, overlaid with the **Add Table** dialog box.

2 In **Add Table**, SELECT **BOOKINGS**, CHOOSE **Add**.

3 SELECT **HOLIDAYS**, CHOOSE **Add**.

4 Close the **Add Table** window.

You need to show Access how the two tables are to be linked for the purposes of this particular query. You do this by linking two fields that now appear in the field lists.

5 Use the field list scroll-bars to adjust the display, so that the **Holiday Number** field name is visible in each. Place the mouse pointer on **Holiday Number** in the **BOOKINGS** field list, then DRAG the mouse over to **Holiday Number** in the **HOLIDAYS** field list and release the button.

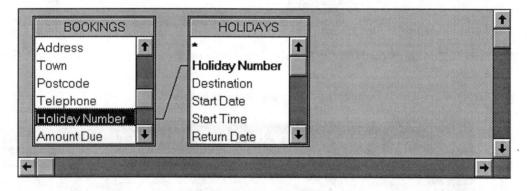

The two related fields become linked, as indicated by the line joining them together. This enables Access to relate the data in one table with the corresponding data in the other.

6 In the lower part of the **Query Design** window, CLICK the **list** button that appears at the top of the first column. CHOOSE **BOOKINGS.Firstname**.

7 CLICK at the top of the second column. A **list** button appears; SELECT the **list** button and CHOOSE **BOOKINGS.Lastname**.

8 CLICK in column three, SELECT the **list** button, CHOOSE **BOOKINGS.Telephone**.

9 CLICK in column four, SELECT the **list** button, use the scroll-bar to display the **HOLIDAYS** fields, CHOOSE **HOLIDAYS.Destination**.

10 SELECT the **Query** menu, CHOOSE **Run**. A dynaset is produced that contains data from both tables.

Firstname	Lastname	Telephone	Destination
Susan	Brown	0205 98765	Le Mans/France
Andrea	Weston	0205 44521	Le Mans/France
Donald	Goodman	0205 33643	Le Mans/France
David	Jackson	0552 32189	Le Mans/France
Paul	McMullan	0529 7737	Coral Sea/Australia
Stella	Wanda	0529 71716	Coral Sea/Australia
Sara	Jones	0476 5567	Athens/Greece
Nancy	Mitchell	0529 8818	Athens/Greece
Mary	Mitchell	0476 2389	Athens/Greece
Edward	Hart	0778 7734	St Tropez/France
Shirley	Robinson	0664 53879	St Tropez/France

Select Query: Query1 — Record: 1

11 SELECT the **File** menu, CHOOSE **Save Query As**; a dialog appears.

12 TYPE **Name and Phone Number by Destination**, CHOOSE **OK** to save the query design.

13 DOUBLE-CLICK the dynaset **Control-menu** box to close the window.

Adding All Fields

At the top of each field list in the query design window there appears an asterisk wildcard; this enables you to add all the fields to your query using one operation. It also has the advantage that, should additional fields be added to the underlying table at a later date, these new fields will be automatically incorporated into the existing query design.

This feature can also be used to make a query that contains all the fields from two (or more) related tables. When designing simple forms and reports, you can use fields from only one table (or dynaset), but you can get around this limitation by using a dynaset that already contains fields from more than one table.

Activity 10.2   Adding all fields from two related tables

1 In the **Database** window SELECT **Query**, CHOOSE **New**. The **Add Table** dialog appears.

2 SELECT **BOOKINGS,** CHOOSE **Add,** SELECT **HOLIDAYS,** CHOOSE **Add.**

3 Close the **Add Table** window.

4 Place the mouse pointer on **Holiday Number** in the **BOOKINGS** field list then DRAG the pointer over to **Holiday Number** in the **HOLIDAYS** field list. The two tables become linked.

5 In the **BOOKINGS** field list DOUBLE-CLICK on the **asterisk** wildcard that appears at the top of the field list.

6 In the **HOLIDAYS** field list DOUBLE-CLICK on the **asterisk** wildcard. The query design appears as follows.

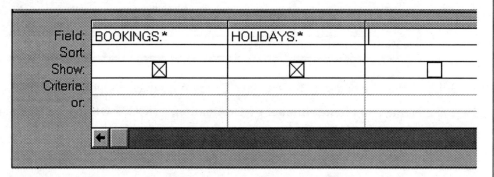

7 CLICK on the **Datasheet View** button (on Toolbar, second from the left); when the query is run, the two wildcards are expanded to display the fields that they represent.

8 SELECT the **File** menu, CHOOSE **Save Query As**; a dialog appears. TYPE **All Fields,** CHOOSE **OK** to save the query design. Keep this query, as we will use it later to create a form.

9 DOUBLE-CLICK the dynaset **Control-menu** box to close the window.

➤ **This task will show you how to copy a query and save it using a different name.**

You may have several similar queries to make. The quickest way to produce a new query is to copy an existing query and then modify the copy.

Activity 11.1 **Making a copy of Bookings for Holiday 3**

1   In the **Database** window SELECT **Query** and then CLICK once on **Bookings for Holiday 3** to select the query name (do not open the query).

2   SELECT the **Edit** menu, CHOOSE **Copy**.

3   SELECT **Edit** menu, CHOOSE **Paste**. The **Paste As** window appears.

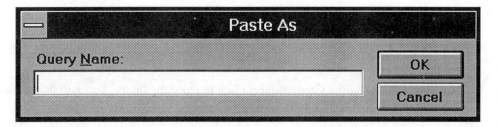

4   TYPE **Addresses for Holiday 3** then CHOOSE **OK**.

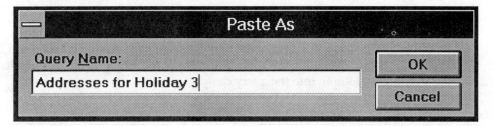

You now have a copy of the query, which is identical to the original except for the name. In the next Activity you will see how to edit the query design to produce an address list.

Task 12 | Editing a query design

➤ **This task will show you how to delete unwanted fields and add new fields to the query design.**

You can change any aspect of the query design. Using the Addresses for Holidays 3 query created in Activity 11.1, you will delete an unwanted field and then add the extra fields required to display the address of each client.

Activity 12.1 **Deleting a field**

1   In the **Database** window SELECT **Query**, SELECT **Addresses for Holiday 3**. CHOOSE the **Design** button.

2   In the lower pane of the **Query Design** window, CLICK anywhere in the **Telephone** column to place the insertion point.

3   SELECT the **Edit** menu, CHOOSE **Delete Column**. The **Telephone** column is deleted from the query design.

4   CHOOSE the **Datasheet View** button; the dynaset now appears without the **Telephone** column.

5   DOUBLE-CLICK on the **Control-menu** box to close the query; you will be prompted to save the change that you have made. CHOOSE **Yes** to make the deletion permanent.

Adding new fields to a query

Here you will add new columns to display the Address, Town and Postcode fields. You will use the 'Drag and Drop' technique as this automatically inserts a new column into the query design.

Activity 12.2 **Adding the Address, Town and Postcode fields to a query**

1   SELECT the **Design** button in the **Database** window.

2   DRAG the **Address** field name from the **BOOKINGS** field list to the **Holiday Number** column. When you release the mouse button, a new column for the **Address** field is inserted into the query design, to the left of **Holiday Number**.

3   Repeat the previous step, but DRAG **Town**.

4   Repeat the previous step, but DRAG **Postcode**.

5 SELECT the **File** menu, CHOOSE **Save**.

6 CHOOSE the **Datasheet View** button to see the result of making this change.

Title	Firstname	Lastname	Town	Address	Postcode
Ms	Sara	Jones	Grantham	195 Malting Rd	GG34 8PD
Mrs	Nancy	Mitchell	Sleaford	15 Harbour Lane	SL3 7CL
Mrs	Mary	Mitchell	York	42 Church Walk	YG3 4CW

Select Query: Addresses for Holiday 3

Record: 1

7 Close the **Select Query** window.

Adding a field from another table

You can add fields from another related table to your query. Here we will add the Holidays table Destination field to the BOOKINGS fields already in Addresses for Holiday 3 query. The tables must be linked using their related fields, so that Access can associate the particular Destination from the HOLIDAYS table with the Holiday Number from the BOOKINGS table.

Activity 12.3 **Adding the Destination field to the Addresses for Holiday 3 query**

1 If necessary, SELECT **Query** in the **Database** window, SELECT **Addresses for Holiday 3**, SELECT the **Design** button to open the query in **Design** view.

2 SELECT the **Query** menu, CHOOSE **Add Table**. The **Add Table** dialog appears.

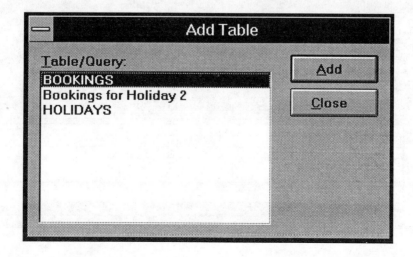

Add Table

Table/Query:
BOOKINGS
Bookings for Holiday 2
HOLIDAYS

Add
Close

3 SELECT **HOLIDAYS**, CHOOSE **Add**; the **HOLIDAYS** field list appears.

4 CHOOSE the Add Table **Close** button.

5 Using the scroll-bars, adjust the view so that the **Holiday Number** field is visible in each list.

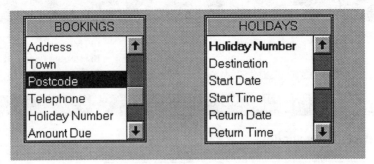

6 DRAG the mouse from one occurrence of **Holiday Number** to the other occurrence (in the other list box). When you release the mouse button, the two tables become linked.

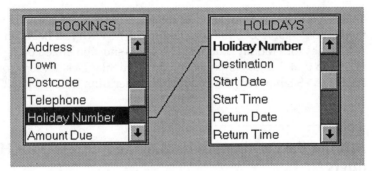

7 DRAG the mouse pointer from the **Destination** field name in **HOLIDAYS** to the **Address** column in the lower pane. A **Destination** column is inserted into the query design.

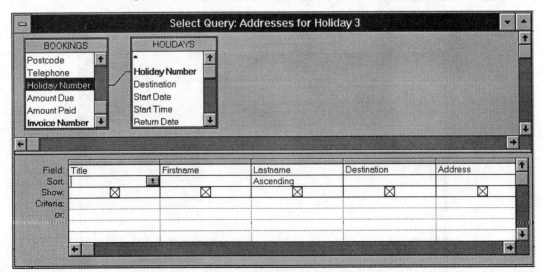

8 SELECT the **File** menu, CHOOSE **Save**.

9 SELECT the **Datasheet View** button to view the result of making these changes; you may need to increase the display width of the **Destination** column.

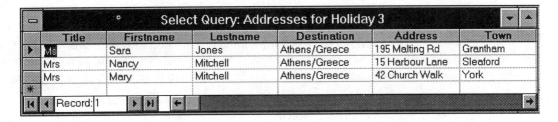

Title	Firstname	Lastname	Destination	Address	Town
Ms	Sara	Jones	Athens/Greece	195 Malting Rd	Grantham
Mrs	Nancy	Mitchell	Athens/Greece	15 Harbour Lane	Sleaford
Mrs	Mary	Mitchell	Athens/Greece	42 Church Walk	York

Select Query: Addresses for Holiday 3

Record: 1

10 Close the **Select Query** window.

Using calculations in a query

> ➤ **This task will show you how to design a query to perform calculations.**

In place of a field name at the top of a column, you can enter an expression (a formula) that will perform a calculation using data from one or more fields in the query. In an expression, field names must be enclosed in square brackets; if the field name does not contain any spaces then Access can add the square brackets for you, but it is a good habit to type them yourself (one less thing to go wrong!).

The computer keyboard lacks keys for the multiply and divide symbols; by convention, an asterisk character ' * ' is used to indicate multiply, whilst a slash '/' is used as a divide symbol.

Activity 13.1 **Calculating the outstanding balances by client**

1 From the **Database** window SELECT **Query**, CHOOSE **New**.

2 SELECT **BOOKINGS**, CHOOSE **Add** from the **Add Table** dialog.

3 Close the **Add Table** window.

4 DOUBLE-CLICK on **Title**, **Firstname**, **Lastname** in the field list.

5 CLICK at the top of the first blank column, to place the insertion point.

6 TYPE **[Amount Due] - [Amount Paid].**

7 CLICK on the **Sort** field in the same column; SELECT the **list** button, CHOOSE **Descending**.

8 SELECT the **File** menu, CHOOSE **Save As**, TYPE **Outstanding Balances**, CHOOSE **OK**.

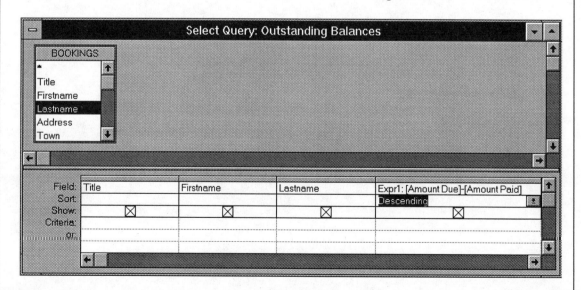

The normal column width is insufficient to display the whole formula. If you need to edit the formula then you can either increase the width of the column or, when you place the insertion point inside the formula, you can use the left and right arrow keys to view any part of the formula.

9   SELECT the **Datasheet View** button to view the dynaset, which appears as follows (in part).

Title	Firstname	Lastname	Expr1
Mrs	Stella	Wanda	£500.00
Mr	Paul	McMullan	£499.00
Ms	Sara	Jones	£145.00
Mrs	Nancy	Mitchell	£145.00
Mrs	Mary	Mitchell	£125.00
Miss	Susan	Brown	£85.00
Ms	Andrea	Weston	£85.00
Mr	Donald	Goodman	£85.00
Mr	David	Jackson	£85.00
Mr	Edward	Hart	£0.00
Mrs	Shirley	Robinson	£0.00

Select Query: Outstanding Balances. Record: 1

The calculated field displays the remaining balance that each client owes to Sunshine Holidays; because it is in descending order, the client who owes the greatest amount appears at the top of the list.

Task 14 Finding records that fall within a range

➤ **This task will show you how to select records that fit inside a range of criteria.**

Activity 14.1 **Producing a list of clients booked on Holidays 2 to 4 (inclusive)**

1 From the **Database** window SELECT **Query**, CHOOSE **New**. SELECT **BOOKINGS**, CHOOSE **Add**. Close the **Add Table** window.

2 DOUBLE-CLICK on **Firstname, Lastname, Telephone, Holiday Number** in the field list.

3 In the **Holidays Number** column CLICK on the **Criteria** field. TYPE **Between 2 AND 4**. CLICK on the **Sort** field, SELECT the **list** button, CHOOSE **Ascending**.

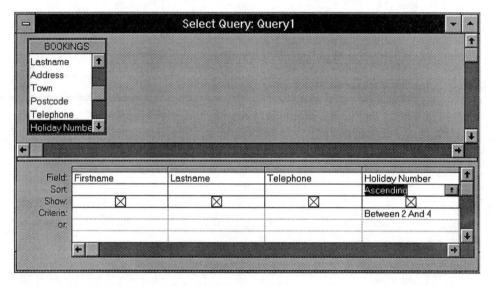

4 SELECT the **Datasheet View** button to view the dynaset.

Firstname	Lastname	Telephone	Holiday Number
Stella	Wanda	0529 71716	2
Paul	McMullan	0529 7737	2
Mary	Mitchell	0476 2389	3
Nancy	Mitchell	0529 8818	3
Sara	Jones	0476 5567	3
Shirley	Robinson	0664 53879	4
Edward	Hart	0778 7734	4
*			0

Record: 1

5 DOUBLE-CLICK the Select Query **Control-menu** box, CHOOSE **No**.

Activity 14.2 **Finding holidays that start in the week beginning Monday 5 July 1993**

1 From the **Database** window SELECT **Query**, CHOOSE **New**.

2 DOUBLE-CLICK on **BOOKINGS**, DOUBLE-CLICK on **HOLIDAYS** in the **Add Table** dialog.

3 SELECT the Add Table **Close** button.

4 DRAG the mouse pointer from **Holiday Number** in the **BOOKINGS** field list onto **Holiday Number** in the **HOLIDAYS** field list. The two tables become linked.

5 DOUBLE-CLICK on **Firstname**, **Lastname**, **Telephone** in the **BOOKINGS** field list.

6 DOUBLE-CLICK on **Destination**, **Start Date** in the **HOLIDAYS** field list.

7 In the **Start Date** column of the QBE grid, CLICK on the **Criteria** field.

8 TYPE **Between 05 Jul 93 and 11 Jul 93.** The query design appears as follows (the width of the **Start Date** column has been increased so that the full expression is displayed).

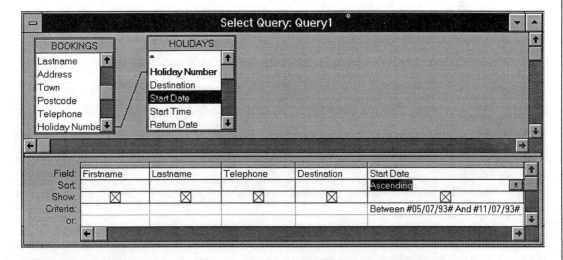

9 SELECT the **Datasheet View** button to view the clients whose holiday begins in the week beginning 5 July 1993.

Firstname	Lastname	Telephone	Destination	Start Date
Stella	Wanda	0529 71716	Coral Sea/Australia	06-Jul-93
Paul	McMullan	0529 7737	Coral Sea/Australia	06-Jul-93
Mary	Mitchell	0476 2389	Athens/Greece	08-Jul-93
Nancy	Mitchell	0529 8818	Athens/Greece	08-Jul-93
Sara	Jones	0476 5567	Athens/Greece	08-Jul-93

Record: 1

10 DOUBLE-CLICK the Select Query window **Control-menu** box, CHOOSE **No**.

| Task 15 | Finding data that corresponds to any one of several values

> ➤ **This task will show you how to select records where the selection criteria is a discontinuous range of values.**

There are two ways of performing this query, which uses the 'or' keyword. You will first use the built-in 'or' fields in the query design, and then show how you can type the selection criteria yourself.

Activity 15.1   **Listing all clients who are booked on Holiday 1 or Holiday 3**

1   From the **Database** window SELECT **Query**, CHOOSE **New**.

2   SELECT **BOOKINGS**, CHOOSE **Add** in the **Add Table** dialog box. Close **Add Table**.

3   DOUBLE-CLICK on **Firstname, Lastname, Telephone, Holiday Number** in the field list.

4   CLICK on the **Criteria** field in the **Holiday Number** column, TYPE **1.**

5   CLICK on the next field (down) in the **Holiday Number** column, TYPE **3**.

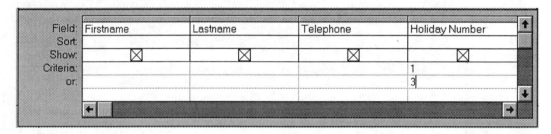

6   CLICK the **Datasheet View** button. The dynaset appears as follows.

	Firstname	Lastname	Telephone	Holiday Number
▶	David	Jackson	0552 32189	1
	Donald	Goodman	0205 33643	1
	Andrea	Weston	0205 44521	1
	Susan	Brown	0205 98765	1
	Mary	Mitchell	0476 2389	3
	Nancy	Mitchell	0529 8818	3
	Sara	Jones	0476 5567	3
				0

Select Query: Query1

Record: 1

An alternative method is to type the select criteria using the 'or' keyword. The following query, in which the criteria 1 or 3 has been entered into the Holiday Number column, produces the same result as previously.

Field:	Firstname	Lastname	Telephone	Holiday Number
Sort:				
Show:	☒	☒	☒	☒
Criteria:				1 or 3
or:				

You can have any number of values in the Criteria field, each separated by the 'or' keyword.

7   DOUBLE-CLICK the Select Query window **Control-menu** box, CHOOSE **No**.

Using the asterisk wildcard in a query

➤ **This task will show you how to use the asterisk wildcard to select a category of records.**

You can use the asterisk wildcard to replace any number of characters in a word. This feature is very flexible and database users often develop great ingenuity in inventing new ways of employing it.

Activity 16.1 **To find all clients who are going to France**

1 From the **Database** window SELECT **Query**, CHOOSE **New**.

2 SELECT **BOOKINGS**, CLICK the **Add** button

3 SELECT **HOLIDAYS**, CLICK the **Add** button. CLICK the Add Table **Close** button.

4 DRAG the mouse pointer from **Holiday Number** in the **BOOKINGS** field list onto **Holiday Number** in the **HOLIDAYS** field list. The two tables become linked.

5 DOUBLE-CLICK on **Firstname**, **Lastname**, **Telephone** in the **BOOKINGS** field list.

6 DOUBLE-CLICK on **Destination** in the **HOLIDAYS** field list.

7 CLICK on the **Criteria** field in the **Destination** column, to place the insertion point.

8 TYPE **＊France**

9 CLICK on the **Sort** field in the **Lastname** column; SELECT the **list** button, CHOOSE **Ascending** to put the dynaset into **Lastname** order. The query design appears as follows.

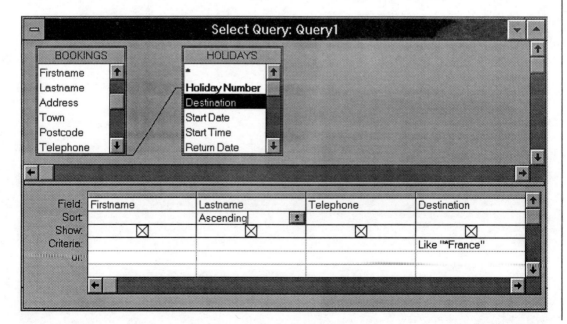

10 CLICK the **Datasheet View** button to view all records where the destination is France.

Firstname	Lastname	Telephone	Destination
Susan	Brown	0205 98765	Le Mans/France
Donald	Goodman	0205 33643	Le Mans/France
Edward	Hart	0778 7734	St Tropez/France
David	Jackson	0552 32189	Le Mans/France
Shirley	Robinson	0664 53879	St Tropez/France
Andrea	Weston	0205 44521	Le Mans/France

Select Query: Query1 — Record: 1

As we have seen, you can use wildcards with the Find command; but it is often better to use them in queries so that, when more than one record matches the criteria, then all the selected records are displayed.

If you look at the criteria field you will see that Access has changed the criteria to: Like "✳France". This is the correct syntax for this query, but if Access recognises the wildcard then it will add the Like keyword for you.

11 DOUBLE-CLICK the Select Query window **Control-menu** box, CHOOSE **No**.

Task 17 | Using parameters in a query

➤ **This task will show you how to create a query that will ask you to enter some information each time the query is used.**

Sometimes you may wish to use a standard query with minor variations. Putting a parameter into a query enables you to enter the selection criteria each time the query is run. A dialog box appears, enabling you to enter the particular criteria to be used on this occasion.

Activity 17.1 **Producing a telephone list of clients booked on any particular holiday**

1   From the **Database** window SELECT **Query**, CHOOSE **New**.

2   SELECT **BOOKINGS**, CLICK the **Add** button in the **Add Table** dialog.

3   Close the **Add Table** window.

4   In the field list, DOUBLE-CLICK on **Firstname**, **Lastname**, **Telephone**, **Holiday Number**.

5   CLICK on the **Criteria** field in the **Holiday Number** column, to place the insertion point.

6   TYPE **[Enter the Holiday Number:]**

7   CLICK the **Datasheet View** button; the **Enter Parameter Value** dialog appears.

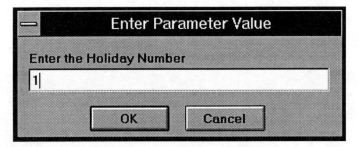

8   TYPE **1** then CHOOSE **OK**. The dynaset appears as follows.

Firstname	Lastname	Telephone	Holiday Number
David	Jackson	0552 32189	1
Donald	Goodman	0205 33643	1
Andrea	Weston	0205 44521	1
Susan	Brown	0205 98765	1
*			0

Record: 1

9　CLICK on **File**, CHOOSE **Save Query As**.

10　TYPE **Bookings by Holiday Number**, CHOOSE **OK**.

11　DOUBLE-CLICK the Select Query window **Control-menu** box, CHOOSE **No**.

The query appears in the Database window when the Query button is selected. You can re-use the query, entering a different Holiday Number each time.

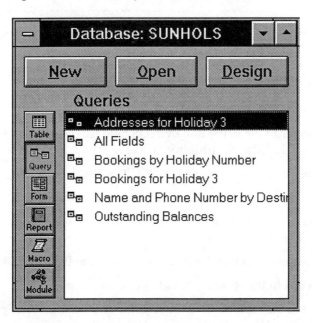

12　CLICK the **Query** button, SELECT **Bookings by Holiday Number**. CHOOSE **Open**.

13　When the **Enter Parameter Value** dialog appears, TYPE **2** then CHOOSE **OK** to produce a dynaset that contains the bookings for **Holiday Number 2**.

14　DOUBLE-CLICK the Select Query window **Control-menu** box, CHOOSE **No**.

➤ This task will show you how to find summary information such as counts and totals.

Activity 18.1 **Finding the total amount due plus a count of the clients booked to go on Holiday 1**

1 From the **Database** window SELECT **Query**, CHOOSE **New**.

2 SELECT **BOOKINGS**, CHOOSE **Add**. Close the **Add Table** window.

3 DOUBLE-CLICK on **Amount Due** in the **BOOKINGS** field list; DOUBLE-CLICK on **Amount Due** in the **BOOKINGS** field list again (this query uses the same field twice).

4 DOUBLE-CLICK on **Holiday Number** in the **BOOKINGS** field list.

5 SELECT the **Sum** button on the Toolbar; a new **Total** row appears in the QBE grid.

6 CLICK on the **Total** row in the first **Amount Due** column to place the insertion point; SELECT the **list** button, CHOOSE **Count**.

7 CLICK on **Total** in the second **Amount Due** column; CLICK the **list** button, CHOOSE **Sum**.

8 CLICK the **Show** check box in the **Holiday Number** column (to uncheck it).

9 CLICK the **Criteria** field in the **Holiday Number** column to place the insertion point, TYPE **1**.

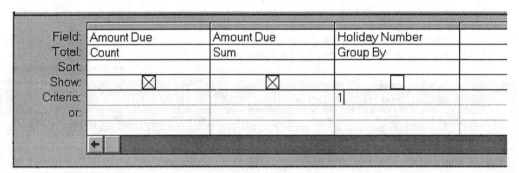

Field:	Amount Due	Amount Due	Holiday Number	
Total:	Count	Sum	Group By	
Sort:				
Show:	☒	☒	☐	
Criteria:			1	
or:				

10 CLICK the **Datasheet View** button to view the dynaset.

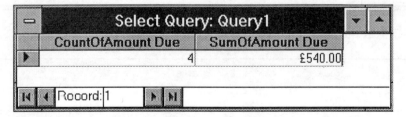

CountOfAmount Due	SumOfAmount Due
4	£540.00

Select Query: Query1 — Record: 1

11 DOUBLE-CLICK the Select Query window **Control-menu** box, CHOOSE **No**.

Activity 18.2 **Finding the number of clients booked on each holiday**

1 SELECT **Query**, CHOOSE **New** from the **Database** window.

2 DOUBLE-CLICK on **BOOKINGS**, DOUBLE-CLICK on **HOLIDAYS** in the **Add Table** dialog. Close the **Add Table** window.

3 DRAG the mouse pointer from **Holiday Number** in the **BOOKINGS** field list onto **Holiday Number** in the **HOLIDAYS** field list. The two tables become linked.

4 SELECT the **list** button at the top of the first column in the QBE grid, CHOOSE **HOLIDAYS.Destination**.

5 CLICK at the top of the next column; a **list** button appears. SELECT the **list** button, CHOOSE **BOOKINGS.Invoice Number**.

6 SELECT the **Sum** button on the Toolbar.

7 CLICK on the **Total** field in the **Invoice Number** column, SELECT the **list** button, CHOOSE **Count**. The QBE grid appears as follows.

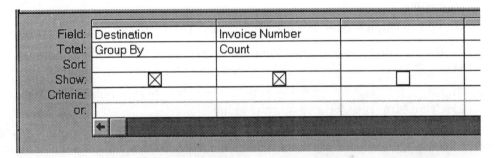

8 SELECT the **File** menu, CHOOSE **Save As**, TYPE **Bookings by Destination**, CHOOSE **OK**.

9 CLICK the **Datasheet View** button; the dynaset appears as follows.

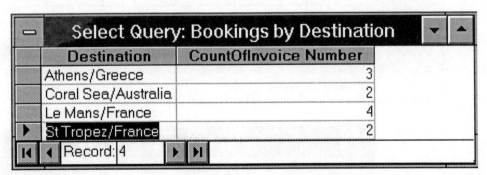

10 DOUBLE-CLICK the Select Query window **Control-menu** box, CHOOSE **No**. Keep this query as it will be used later to show how data from a table or query can be incorporated into a chart.

Finding the maximum and minimum values

You can design your query so that the resulting dynaset is sorted using the data in any particular field. This is one way of finding maximum and minimum values, and has the advantage that other fields can provide information such as the name and telephone number of the client who owes the greatest amount of money. If you just wish to find the maximum and minimum values in a table column, you can use the Max and Min functions.

Activity 18.3 **Find the maximum and minimum amount due from Sunshine Holidays clients**

1 SELECT **Query**, CHOOSE **New** from the **Database** window.

2 DOUBLE-CLICK on **BOOKINGS** in the **Add Table** dialog box. CHOOSE **Close**.

3 DOUBLE-CLICK on **Amount Due** in the **BOOKINGS** field list; DOUBLE-CLICK on **Amount Due** again.

4 SELECT the **Sum** button on the Toolbar; a new **Total** row appears in the query definition.

5 CLICK the **Total** row in the first **Amount Due** column, SELECT the **list** button, CHOOSE **Max**.

6 CLICK on the **Total** row in the second **Amount Due** column, SELECT the **list** button, CHOOSE **Min**. The QBE grid appears as follows.

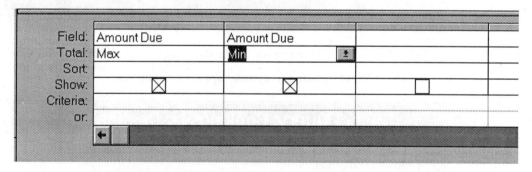

7 CLICK the **Datasheet View** button. The dynaset appears as follows.

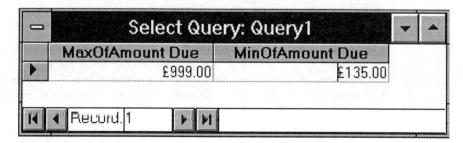

8 Close the **Query** window.

Bringing it all together

➤ **This task will show you how to use several techniques in the same query.**

Here you will design a query that incorporates several of the features that you have used singly. It uses a parameter and a calculation as selection criteria; the records to be selected are those for which the Holiday Number is the same as the parameter entered when the query is run, *and* where the outstanding balance is greater than zero.

Keep this query, as it is used later to produce a report.

Activity 19.1 **Finding outstanding balances**

1   From the **Database** window SELECT **Query**, CHOOSE **New**. The **Query Design** form appears, overlaid with the **Add Table** dialog box.

2   In **Add Table**, DOUBLE-CLICK on **BOOKINGS**, DOUBLE-CLICK on **HOLIDAYS**. SELECT the Add Table **Close** button.

3   DRAG the mouse pointer from **Holiday Number** in the **BOOKINGS** field list onto **Holiday Number** in the **HOLIDAYS** field list. The two tables become linked.

4   In the **BOOKINGS** field list DOUBLE-CLICK on: **Title, Firstname, Lastname, Address, Town, Postcode, Holiday Number, Amount Due, Amount Paid, Invoice Number.**

5   In the **HOLIDAYS** field list DOUBLE-CLICK on: **Destination, Start Date, Return Date.**

6   CLICK on the **Criteria** field in the **Holiday Number** column, to place the insertion point.

7   TYPE **[Enter the Holiday Number]**.

8   CLICK anywhere in the **Invoice Number** column to place the insertion point.

9   SELECT the **Edit** menu, CHOOSE **Insert Column**. A new blank column appears to the left of the **Invoice Number** column.

10 CLICK at the top of the new column to place the insertion point.

11 TYPE **BALANCE:[Amount Due] - [Amount Paid]**.

12 CLICK on the **Criteria** field in the **Amount Due** column, to place the insertion point.

13 TYPE **[Amount Due] - [Amount Paid] > 0**.

14 SELECT the **File** menu, CHOOSE **Save As**. TYPE **Outstanding Balances**, SELECT **OK**.

15 CHOOSE **Yes** to replace the previous query of the same name (this one is more sophisticated). The query design appears as follows (in part).

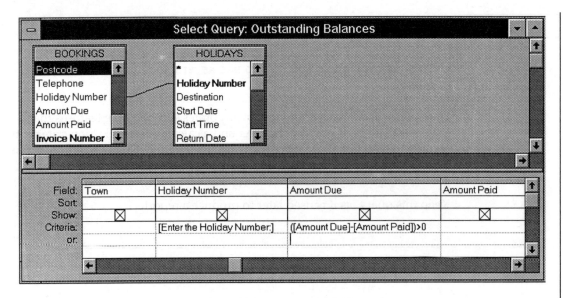

16 SELECT the **Datasheet View** button; the **Enter Parameter Value** dialog box appears.

17 TYPE **3**, SELECT **OK**. The dynaset appears as follows (in part).

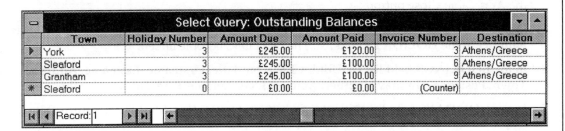

18 Re-run the query and this time enter **Holiday Number 4**. There are no outstanding balances owed by the clients booked on this holiday, and the dynaset appears as follows (in part).

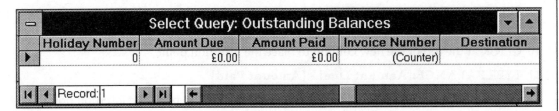

19 DOUBLE-CLICK the Select Query window **Control-menu** box to close the window.

Section C
Updating the data in a table

Task 20: To add, update and delete a record
Task 21: To edit data in a dynaset
Task 22: To edit data in linked tables
Task 23: To use an action query

Task 20 Keeping your data up-to-date

➤ **This task will show you how to add, edit and delete a record.**

The last row of the table is always kept blank, as indicated by the asterisk that appears on the row selector. It is ready for you to enter data.

Activity 20.1 **Adding a new record**

1 SELECT **BOOKINGS** in the **Database** window, CHOOSE **Open**.

2 CLICK on the first field of the last row to place the insertion point, TYPE **Miss**, PRESS **Tab**. A pencil symbol appears on the row selector to indicate that the data has not yet been saved.

3 Repeat for the following data items: **Zoe, Silverman, 88 Sunny Ave, Boston, BT9 9PD, 0205 87654, 2, 999, 450.**

Title	Firstname	Lastname	Address	Town	Postcode
Mrs	Stella	Wanda	18 Cherry Grove	Sleaford	SL18 7TT
Mr	David	Jackson	16 Georges St	Lincoln	LN6 8GS
Mrs	Mary	Mitchell	42 Church Walk	York	YG3 4CW
Mr	Donald	Goodman	12 Ruskin Lane	Boston	BT34 8QT
Ms	Andrea	Weston	Opal Cottage	Boston	BT5 8SC
Mrs	Nancy	Mitchell	15 Harbour Lane	Sleaford	SL3 7CL
Mrs	Shirley	Robinson	12 Dickens Lane	Melton	MN2 9DL
Mr	Paul	McMullan	102 Grant Rd	Sleaford	SL3 4GR
Ms	Sara	Jones	195 Malting Rd	Grantham	GG34 8PD
Miss	Susan	Brown	11 Dickens St	Boston	BT8 8QT
Mr	Edward	Hart	68 Hunters Lane	Redmond	WG5 2HV
Miss	Zoe	Silverman	88 Sunny Ave	Boston	BT9 9PD

Table: BOOKINGS

Record: 12

4 PRESS ⬚Tab⬚ to move the insertion point on; the **Invoice Number** is generated automatically. A new blank row is appended to the table, ready for you to enter more data. The new data is saved automatically when the insertion point is moved out of the row (or when you close the **Table** window).

Editing the data

Normally, whilst viewing a table, pressing the left and right arrow keys causes the insertion point or highlight to move from one field to the next. To edit the data in a field, first click on that field to place the insertion point and then use the arrow keys to move the insertion point through the data.

Activity 20.2 **Editing the data in a record**

1 CLICK on the **Amount Paid** field in Miss Silverman's record, just to the right of the data.

2 PRESS ⬚Backspace⬚ to delete the current entry.

3 TYPE **999** and PRESS ⬚Tab⬚. The new data is automatically saved when the insertion point is moved out of the row, or when you close the window.

Activity 20.3 **Deleting a record**

1 CLICK on the **row selector** for Miss Silverman's record (the row selectors are the plain grey buttons immediately to the left of the **Title** column). The row becomes highlighted.

Title	Firstname	Lastname	Address	Town	Postcode
Mrs	Stella	Wanda	18 Cherry Grove	Sleaford	SL18 7TT
Mr	David	Jackson	16 Georges St	Lincoln	LN6 8GS
Mrs	Mary	Mitchell	42 Church Walk	York	YG3 4CW
Mr	Donald	Goodman	12 Ruskin Lane	Boston	BT34 8QT
Ms	Andrea	Weston	Opal Cottage	Boston	BT5 8SC
Mrs	Nancy	Mitchell	15 Harbour Lane	Sleaford	SL3 7CL
Mrs	Shirley	Robinson	12 Dickens Lane	Melton	MN2 9DL
Mr	Paul	McMullan	102 Grant Rd	Sleaford	SL3 4GR
Ms	Sara	Jones	195 Malting Rd	Grantham	GG34 8PD
Miss	Susan	Brown	11 Dickens St	Boston	BT8 8QT
Mr	Edward	Hart	68 Hunters Lane	Redmond	WG5 2HV
Miss	Zoe	Silverman	88 Sunny Ave	Boston	BT9 9PD

Table: BOOKINGS

Record: 12

2 SELECT the **Edit** menu, CHOOSE **Delete**. A dialog box appears. CHOOSE **OK** to confirm the deletion. Close the **Table** window.

Using a dynaset to edit a table

> ➤ **This task will show you how to edit the data in the dynaset. The table that the data was extracted from will be automatically updated to reflect the changes that you make.**

Activity 21.1 **Using a dynaset to update data**

1   From the **Database** window, SELECT the **Query** button, SELECT **Bookings for Holiday 3**, CHOOSE **Open**. The query is executed to produce a dynaset.

2   CLICK on the **Title** field for Ms Jones to place the insertion point, PRESS Backspace to delete the existing entry, TYPE **Mrs**.

3   PRESS Tab to move the insertion point into the **Lastname** field, PRESS Backspace to delete Jones, TYPE **Floyd** (because Miss Jones is now married to a Mr Floyd).

4   DOUBLE-CLICK on the **Control-menu** box to close the dynaset window; the changes that you have made to the data are saved automatically. You can open the query to check this; the dynaset appears as follows.

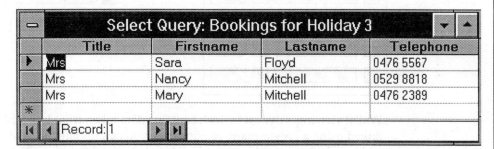

5   Edit this dynaset to reverse the previous changes.

6   Close the dynaset window.

Task 22 Editing the data in linked tables

➤ **This task will show you how to edit the data in one of the two related fields used to link tables; the other related field is updated automatically.**

When you use a query to view data from two linked tables, Access links each row in the 'many' table with the corresponding row in the primary table (in which the related field is a primary key, and cannot contain duplicate entries).

When you edit the query, such that the existing link is no longer valid, Access will automatically make a new link with the appropriate row in the second table. For example, if a client decided to cancel his booking for Holiday 2, and instead to go on Holiday 3, the link is re-made.

BOOKINGS   **HOLIDAYS**

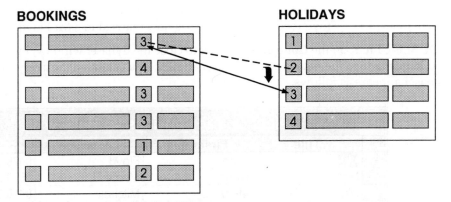

Whilst viewing a dynaset which contains data taken from two tables which are linked using a one-to-many relationship, you can update the related field in the table on the 'many' side. A new link is automatically set up with the appropriate row in the 'one' table.

Activity 22.1 **Editing the linked field in a dynaset containing data from two related tables**

1   In the **Database** window SELECT **Query**, CHOOSE **New**.

2   SELECT **BOOKINGS**, CHOOSE **Add**, SELECT **HOLIDAYS**, CHOOSE **Add**.

3   Close the **Add Table** window.

4   Place the mouse pointer on **Holiday Number** in the **BOOKINGS** list box then DRAG the pointer over to **Holiday Number** in the **HOLIDAYS** list box. The two tables become linked.

5   In the **BOOKINGS** field list DOUBLE-CLICK on **Firstname**, **Lastname**, **Holiday Number**.

6 In the **HOLIDAYS** list box DOUBLE-CLICK on **Destination**.

7 CLICK on the **Datasheet View** button. The dynaset generated by the query appears as follows (in part).

Firstname	Lastname	Holiday Number	Destination
Susan	Brown	1	Le Mans/France
Andrea	Weston	1	Le Mans/France
Donald	Goodman	1	Le Mans/France
David	Jackson	1	Le Mans/France
Paul	McMullan	2	Coral Sea/Australia
Stella	Wanda	2	Coral Sea/Australia
Sara	Jones	3	Athens/Greece

Select Query: Query1

8 CLICK on the **Holiday Number** in Sara Jones' row, to place the insertion point.

9 PRESS ⎡Del⎤ to delete the current entry, TYPE **4**.

10 PRESS any ⎡**arrow key**⎤ to move the insertion point into another field. The whole record is updated to reflect any changes. You will see the **Destination** field change to match the **Holiday Number**. The dynaset now appears as follows.

Firstname	Lastname	Holiday Number	Destination
Susan	Brown	1	Le Mans/France
Andrea	Weston	1	Le Mans/France
Donald	Goodman	1	Le Mans/France
David	Jackson	1	Le Mans/France
Paul	McMullan	2	Coral Sea/Australia
Stella	Wanda	2	Coral Sea/Australia
Sara	Jones	4	St Tropez/France

Select Query: Query1

11 DOUBLE-CLICK the dynaset **Control-menu** box to close the window. CHOOSE **No** (because you do not want to save the query design).

12 SELECT **Table** in the **Database** window.

13 DOUBLE-CLICK on **BOOKINGS**. When the **BOOKINGS** table appears, you will see that this has been updated too.

14 DOUBLE-CLICK the BOOKINGS table **Control-menu** box to close this window.

Task 23 Using action queries

➤ **This task will show you how to design and safely test an action query before using it to update some records in a table.**

This is a type of query that, instead of listing records, will update or delete the selected records. Because of the potential for large scale changes to be made to the data whilst experimenting with action queries, you will use BOOKINGS-Experiments, a copy of the BOOKINGS table made in Activities 8.2 and 8.3.

This method is especially useful for changing the price charged to a group; here you will add £10 to the Amount Due field for all holidays that go to France.

If you are very confident, then you can design your update query and run it; but here you will check that the query is working as expected before using it to update the table. You will first design a normal query that displays the new prices and the destination. If this is OK (all the destinations are in France, for example) then you will convert the query into an action query.

Currently, the Amount Due column appears as follows.

Telephone	Holiday Number	Amount Due	Amount Paid	Invoice Number
0529 71716	2	£999.00	£499.00	1
0552 32189	1	£135.00	£50.00	2
0476 2389	3	£245.00	£120.00	3
0205 33643	1	£135.00	£50.00	4
0205 44521	1	£135.00	£50.00	5
0529 8818	3	£245.00	£100.00	6
0664 53879	4	£295.00	£295.00	7
0529 7737	2	£999.00	£500.00	8
0476 5567	3	£245.00	£100.00	9
0205 98765	1	£135.00	£50.00	10
0778 7734	4	£295.00	£295.00	11
	0	£0.00	£0.00	(Counter)

Table: BOOKINGS-Experiments

Record: 12

Activity 23.1 **Adding £10 to the Amount Due for all French holidays**

1 From the **Database** window, SELECT **Query**, CHOOSE **New**.

2 In the **Add Table** dialog box SELECT **BOOKINGS-Experiments** and CHOOSE **Add**. SELECT **HOLIDAYS** and CHOOSE **Add**. CHOOSE the **Close** button.

3 DRAG the mouse from **Holiday Number** in the **BOOKINGS-Experiments** field list to the **Holiday Number** in the **HOLIDAYS** field list. The tables become linked.

4 DOUBLE-CLICK on **Amount Due** in the **BOOKINGS-Experiments** field list; the field name appears in the first column of the query design.

5 CLICK at the top of the second column of the QBE grid to place the insertion point.

6 TYPE **[Amount Due] + 10** and PRESS Enter .

7 DOUBLE-CLICK on **Holiday Number** in the **BOOKINGS-Experiments** field list; the field name appears in the query design.

8 In the **Holiday Number** column TYPE **1 Or 4** in the **Criteria** row (the **Holiday Numbers** of the two tours that go to France). CLICK the **Show** check box (to uncheck it).

9 DOUBLE-CLICK on **Destination** in the **HOLIDAYS** field list; the field name appears in the query design, which appears similar to the following.

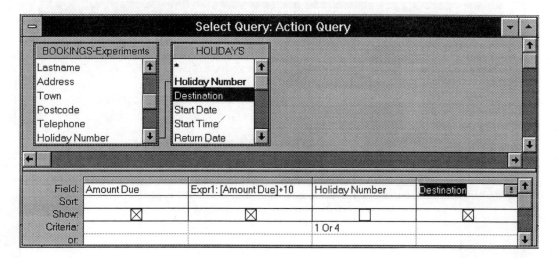

10 CLICK the **Datasheet View** button; the dynaset appears as follows.

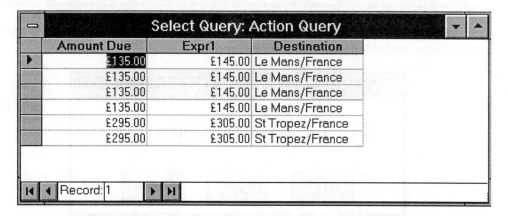

11 Having checked that the query produces the correct dynaset, SELECT the **Design** button to return to **Design** view.

12 SELECT the **Query** menu, CHOOSE **Update** to convert the query into an update query. Access removes the **Sort** and **Show** rows from the query design (because they are no longer relevant) and adds a new **Update To** row.

13 DRAG the mouse across the formula in the top field of the second column (omit the **Expr1:** name added by Access). The formula becomes highlighted.

14 SELECT the **Edit** menu, CHOOSE **Copy**.

15 CLICK on the **Update To** field of the **Amount Due** column, to place the insertion point.

16 SELECT the **Edit** menu, CHOOSE **Paste**.

17 You no longer need the original calculated field. DRAG the mouse pointer across the formula **Expr1** to select it, SELECT the **Edit** menu, CHOOSE **Delete**.

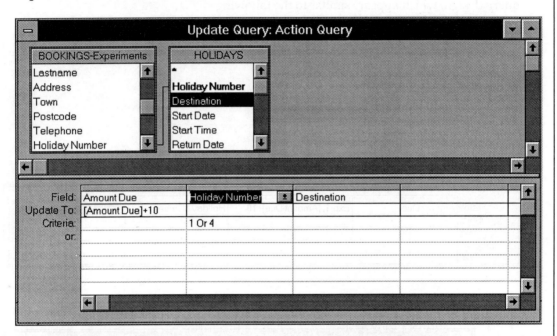

18 SELECT the **Query** menu, CHOOSE **Run** (or use the **Query Run** button on the Toolbar). A dialog appears, asking you to confirm the update.

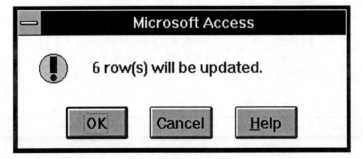

19 CHOOSE **OK**. The update query is executed.

20 DOUBLE-CLICK on the Query **Control-menu** box to close the window, CHOOSE **No**, (because you do not want to save the query design).

21 From the **Database** window SELECT the **BOOKINGS-Experiments** table and CHOOSE **Open** to view the changes made by the update query.

Telephone	Holiday Number	Amount Due	Amount Paid	Invoice Number
0529 71716	2	£999.00	£499.00	1
0552 32189	1	£145.00	£50.00	2
0476 2389	3	£245.00	£120.00	3
0205 33643	1	£145.00	£50.00	4
0205 44521	1	£145.00	£50.00	5
0529 8818	3	£245.00	£100.00	6
0664 53879	4	£305.00	£295.00	7
0529 7737	2	£999.00	£500.00	8
0476 5567	3	£245.00	£100.00	9
0205 98765	1	£145.00	£50.00	10
0778 7734	4	£305.00	£295.00	11
	0	£0.00	£0.00	(Counter)

Table: BOOKINGS-Experiments

Record: 12

22 Close the **Table** window.

Saving the query

If you had used this query on a 'real' table of business data then you would probably not need to use the same update again, but you could save the query and re-use it with a different holiday and price increase. In the Database window you would select the query name and choose the Design button to view the query design; you would then edit the query design to change the Holiday Number and the amount to be added to the Amount Due, and run the modified update query.

However, if other people are going to use your database, this query may be a dangerous one to keep on the database - someone else may run it to see what it does!

Delete queries

A delete query is a type of action query. The only entries that you need to place into the QBE grid are the fields used as selection criteria. To convert the select query into a delete query, select the Query menu and choose Delete.

There is no way to recover deleted records (other than from a backup copy of the database).

Needless to say, this type of query can be very destructive!

Section D

Restructuring a table

Task 24: To add a field and enter data; then move, rename and delete a field
Task 25: To declare a default value for a field

Task 24   Modifying the table design

➤ **This task will show you how to add another field to an existing table, enter data and then move, rename and delete the field.**

When you begin using a database you often find that you need to add another field, or make an existing field longer. Occasionally, you may wish to rename a field, change the position it occupies when the datasheet is displayed, or delete an unwanted field. All of these things are easily accomplished.

When the length of a field has been increased, you may need to edit the design of any forms or reports that display this field; the only change necessary is to select the field and then drag the right-hand edge of the field to the right, to make it large enough to display the increased amount of data.

Activity 24.1   **Adding a second telephone field to BOOKINGS**

1   From the **Database** window CHOOSE **Table**, SELECT **BOOKINGS**, CHOOSE **Design**. The **Table Design** window appears.

2   CLICK on **Holiday Number**, SELECT the **Edit** menu, CHOOSE **Insert Row**. A blank row appears above the **Holiday Number** field.

3   TYPE **Telephone 2** and PRESS Tab . The field is already set to have the default data type 'Text' (which we want). The **Field Properties** box appears.

4   CLICK on the **Field Size** field, PRESS Backspace to delete the current entry, TYPE **10**.

5   SELECT the **File** menu, CHOOSE **Save**.

6   SELECT **Datasheet View**.

Activity 24.2 Entering data into the new Telephone 2 field

1 CLICK on the first field of the **Telephone 2** column to place the insertion point.

2 TYPE **0123 6666** and PRESS the | **Down arrow** | key.

3 TYPE **0123 7777** and PRESS the | **Down arrow** | key.

4 TYPE **0123 8888**.

5 DOUBLE-CLICK the Table window **Control-menu** box to close the window (the new data is saved automatically).

Renaming a field

Often, after creating a field, you think of a more descriptive field name; it is easy to rename a field in Access.

Activity 24.3 Renaming the two Telephone fields to be Telephone (Home) and Telephone (Day)

1 In the **Database** window, SELECT the **Table** button, CHOOSE **Design**.

2 CLICK at the right-hand side of the field name **Telephone 2** to place the insertion point.

3 PRESS | **Backspace** | to delete the **2**.

4 TYPE **(Day)**.

5 CLICK at the right-hand side of the field name **Telephone**.

6 TYPE a **Space** then TYPE **(Home)**.

7 SELECT the **File** menu, CHOOSE **Save**.

8 Close the **Table Design** window.

Moving a field

When using a database, you often want the most useful fields to appear at the left of the table. Moving a field in the Table Design window will change the column order when you view the data. This 'Drag and Drop' operation is easy to perform but many people find it a bit fiddly to do at first.

Activity 24.4   **Moving Telephone (Home) to appear before Telephone (Day)**

1   In the **Database** window, SELECT **BOOKINGS**, CHOOSE the **Design** button. The **Table Design** window appears.

2   SELECT the **row selector** for **Telephone (Day)**; the row becomes highlighted.

Table: BOOKINGS		
Field Name	**Data Type**	**Description**
Title	Text	
Firstname	Text	
Lastname	Text	
Address	Text	
Town	Text	
Postcode	Text	
Telephone (Home)	Text	
Telephone (Day)	Text	
Holiday Number	Number	
Amount Due	Currency	
Amount Paid	Currency	
Invoice Number	Counter	

3   Place the pointer on the row selector; PRESS and HOLD DOWN the mouse button. Access displays a thin white horizontal bar just above the selected row.

4   DRAG the horizontal bar up and onto the field name **Telephone (Home)**; release the mouse button. **Telephone (Day)** appears in its new position, above **Telephone (Home)**.

5   SELECT the **File** menu, CHOOSE **Save**.

6   Close the **Table Design** window.

Changing the field size

When you enter data, you sometimes encounter an item that is too long to fit into its field; this is most likely to happen with people and place names. Here you will increase the length of the Town field to accommodate such places as 'Royal Tunbridge Wells' that are longer than the current field size of 20 characters (remember that a space counts as a character).

If you increase the field size, any existing data will be unaffected, but if you decrease the field size, when you save the query design, you will see a message warning you that data may be lost. In fact, only data items longer than the (now reduced) field size are affected - these are truncated to fit inside the smaller field.

Activity 24.5   **Increasing the size of the Town field to 24 characters**

1   In the **Database** window, SELECT **Table**, SELECT **BOOKINGS**, CHOOSE **Design**.

2   CLICK on the **Town** field name; the **Field Properties** section becomes active.

3   CLICK on the **Field Size** field in the **Field Properties** box to place the insertion point. Delete the existing entry, TYPE **24**.

4   SELECT the **File** menu, CHOOSE **Save**.

5   Close the **Table Design** window.

Activity 24.6   **Deleting the Telephone (Day) field**

When you delete a field, any data it contains will be lost.

1   In the **Database** window, SELECT **Table**, SELECT **BOOKINGS**, CHOOSE **Design**.

2   SELECT the Telephone (Day) field **row selector** button; the row becomes highlighted.

3   SELECT the **Edit** menu, CHOOSE **Delete**.

4   A dialog appears; CHOOSE **OK** to confirm. The field is deleted from the **Table Design**.

5   SELECT the **File** menu, CHOOSE **Save**.

6   Close the **Table Design** window.

Task 25 Setting a default value

➤ **This task will show you how to set a default value for a field.**

If you frequently enter identical data into a field, you can speed data entry by specifying that data value as a default value. Access will then enter that value automatically whenever you enter a new record. For example, if your travel company is located in Sleaford, and many of your clients live in that town, you may wish to set a default value of 'Sleaford' for the Town field.

Activity 25.1   **Setting Sleaford as a default value for the Town field**

1   SELECT **BOOKINGS** in the **Database** window, CHOOSE **Design**.

2   CLICK on the **Town** field name; the **Field Properties** section becomes active.

3   CLICK on the **Default Value** field to place the insertion point.

4   TYPE **Sleaford**.

5   SELECT the **File** menu, CHOOSE **Save**.

6   SELECT the **Datasheet View** button to view the table.

Title	Firstname	Lastname	Address	Town	Postcode
Mrs	Stella	Wanda	18 Cherry Grove	Sleaford	SL18 7TT
Mr	David	Jackson	16 Georges St	Lincoln	LN6 8GS
Mrs	Mary	Mitchell	42 Church Walk	York	YG3 4CW
Mr	Donald	Goodman	12 Ruskin Lane	Boston	BT34 8QT
Ms	Andrea	Weston	Opal Cottage	Boston	BT5 8SC
Mrs	Nancy	Mitchell	15 Harbour Lane	Sleaford	SL3 7CL
Mrs	Shirley	Robinson	12 Dickens Lane	Melton	MN2 9DL
Mr	Paul	McMullan	102 Grant Rd	Sleaford	SL3 4GR
Ms	Sara	Jones	195 Malting Rd	Grantham	GG34 8PD
Miss	Susan	Brown	11 Dickens St	Boston	BT8 8QT
Mr	Edward	Hart	68 Hunters Lane	Redmond	WG5 2HV
				Sleaford	

Table: BOOKINGS

Record: 12

As usual, the last row is blank, ready for you to enter a new record. Sleaford has already been entered into the Town field. If your next client is from Sleaford, just press Tab to move the insertion point into the next field. If the client is from another town, you can type the Town data as usual.

Section E
Working with forms

Task 26: To use a Wizard to create a form
Task 27: To view and update records in Form View
Task 28: To create a form using fields from two tables
Task 29: To customise a form
Task 30: To display a picture using a form
Task 31: To add a chart to a form

Task 26 Creating a form

➤ **This task will show you how to use a FormWizard to create a form.**

Forms enable you to view data in a customised layout; enable you to view only those fields relevant to the task in hand, and help you concentrate on the information in a single record. To create a form you should use the FormWizard which will ask you to choose some options and then create the form for you.

Activity 26.1   **Creating a new form using the FormWizard**

1   In the **Database** window SELECT the **Form** button, CHOOSE **New**.

2   The **New Form** dialog appears; SELECT the **list** button, CHOOSE **BOOKINGS**.

---

3   CHOOSE the **FormWizards** button. There are different Wizards for different types of form; the single-column default option (which we want) is already selected.

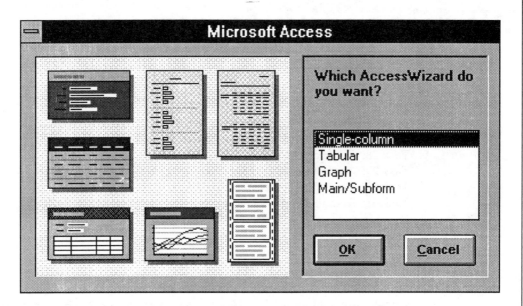

4   CHOOSE **OK**. The **FormWizard** dialog appears.

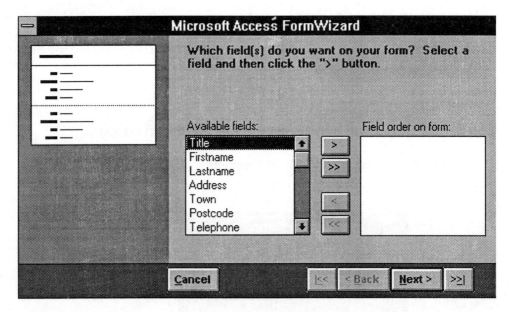

5   CLICK the '>>' button to move all the fields into the **Field order on form** list.

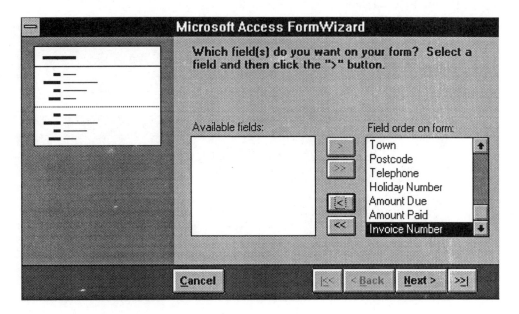

6   CLICK the **Next>** button.

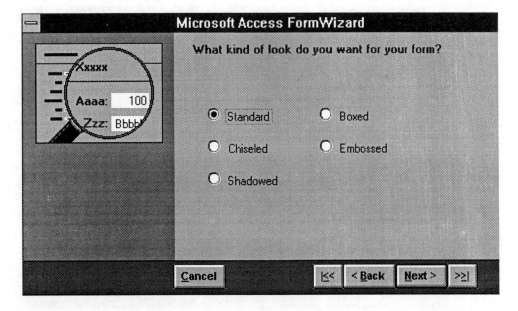

7   The **FormWizard** offers several options for how the form will appear on-screen. **Standard** is already selected. CHOOSE **Next>**.

8 Optionally, you can type a title that will appear at the top of the form; here we will accept the default name **BOOKINGS**.

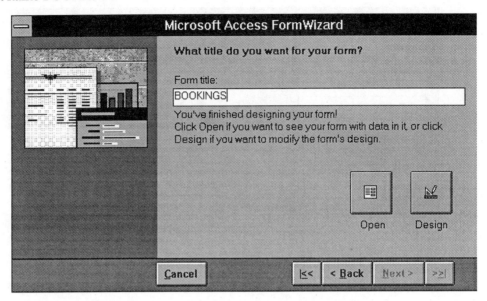

9 CHOOSE **Open**. The form appears, displaying the data from the **BOOKINGS** table.

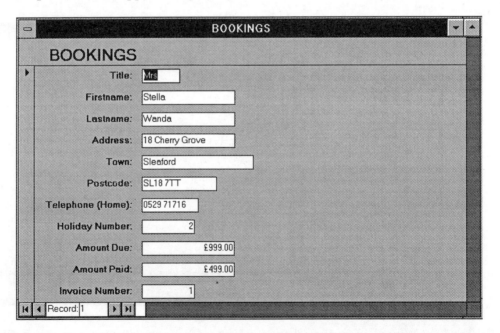

10 SELECT the **File** menu, CHOOSE **Save Form As**, type **BOOKINGS**, CHOOSE **OK.** The name used here is the same as the form title as this makes it easier to remember what it does; the name does not have to be the same. Form naming rules are given in **Task 2.**

11 Close the **Form** window.

Task 27 | Viewing and updating records

➤ **This task will show you how to view, add, update or delete a record in form view.**

Because a form usually enables you to view all the fields of one record, it is often convenient to use forms to browse and edit your data.

Activity 27.1 Browsing through records using a form

1 In the **Database** window SELECT the **Form** button, SELECT **BOOKINGS**, CHOOSE **Open**.

2 Now you can browse through the records using the VCR-like navigation controls, in the same way as when browsing in **Table** view.

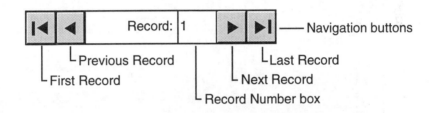

Activity 27.2 Adding a new record

1 CLICK the **Last Record** button in the navigation controls.

2 CLICK the **Next record** button. A blank form appears.

3 TYPE **Mr** and then PRESS Tab .

4 TYPE **John** and then PRESS Tab .

5 Repeat for these items of information: **Marsh, 77 Orange Grove.**

6 PRESS Tab to accept the default **Town** value of Sleaford.

7 TYPE the following items of information and PRESS Tab after each: **SL8 8TY, 0529 88888, 2, 999.00, 499.00.**

8 When the insertion point enters the **Invoice Number** field, PRESS Tab to move the insertion point on. This number is generated automatically.

9 Another blank form appears, enabling you to enter another record if you wish. When you have no more records to enter, close the form window; the new data is saved automatically.

Activity 27.3   Editing the data

1   Open the **BOOKINGS** form, use the navigation controls to display the record for **John Marsh**.

2   CLICK on the **Title** field to place the insertion point.

3   PRESS ⌷Backspace⌷ to delete the existing entry.

4   TYPE **Rev**.

5   CLICK on the **Previous Record** button to move the insertion point out of this record.

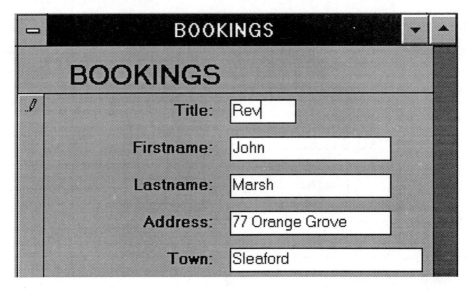

When you edit a record, a pencil symbol appears on the left of the form to indicate that the new data has not been saved. When you view another record, or close the form, the changes are then saved automatically.

Activity 27.4   Deleting a record

1   Use the navigation controls to display the record for **John Marsh**.

2   SELECT the vertical bar on the left side of the form; the bar becomes highlighted. Alternatively, you can SELECT the **Edit** menu and CHOOSE **Select Record.**

3   SELECT the **Edit** menu, CHOOSE **Delete**.

4   CHOOSE **OK** to confirm the deletion.

5   Close the **BOOKINGS** form window.

Task 28 | Displaying fields from multiple tables

> ➤ **This task will show you how to design a form that displays fields from two tables.**

When using the FormWizard to create a simple form, you can incorporate fields from only one table into the form design.

There is a way round this limitation. Your form can incorporate fields from a dynaset (a type of table) which itself has been produced using a query design that contains all the required fields from these tables. The tables must be linked together using the data in their related fields.

Here you will create a form based on the dynaset produced by the All Fields query that was created in Activity 11.3.

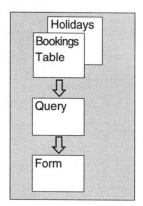

Activity 28.1 **Creating a form that displays fields chosen from both HOLIDAYS and BOOKINGS**

1 In the **Database** window SELECT the **Form** button, CHOOSE **New**. The **New Form** dialog appears.

2 SELECT the Combo box **list** button, CHOOSE **All Fields**.

3 CHOOSE the **FormWizards** button. A new dialog appears; the single-column default option is already selected.

4 CHOOSE **OK**. The **FormWizard** dialog appears.

5 SELECT **Title**, CLICK the '>' button to move the **Title** field into the **Field order on form** list.

6 In turn, SELECT the following fields and CLICK the '>' button to move the field into the **Field order on form** list: **Firstname, Lastname, BOOKINGS.Holiday Number, Destination**.

7 CLICK the **Next>** button.

8 CHOOSE **Next>** to use the (already selected) **Standard** form appearence.

9 TYPE **DESTINATIONS** as the form title.

10 CHOOSE **Open**. The newly created form appears, displaying data from the first record in the database.

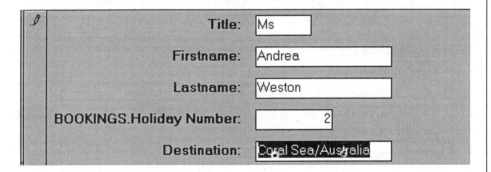

Title:	Ms
Firstname:	Andrea
Lastname:	Weston
BOOKINGS.Holiday Number:	1
Destination:	Le Mans/France

11 SELECT **File**, CHOOSE **Save Form As**, type **Client plus Destination**, CHOOSE **OK**.

Activity 28.2   Editing the related fields

1   CLICK on the **BOOKINGS.Holiday Number** field to place the insertion point.

2   PRESS `Del` to delete the existing entry, TYPE **2**. PRESS `Enter` to move the insertion point into the next field. The value displayed in the **Destination** field changes automatically to match the new **Holiday Number**.

Title:	Ms
Firstname:	Andrea
Lastname:	Weston
BOOKINGS.Holiday Number:	2
Destination:	Coral Sea/Australia

If you were to close the form window at this point, the BOOKINGS table would be updated to show Andrea booked onto Holiday Number 2.

3   CLICK on the **Destination** field to place the insertion point.

4   Attempt to delete the existing entry; Access will not let you do this, because changing the destination for this record would (logically but perhaps unintentionally) change the destination for all clients booked to go on the same Holiday Number.

5   CLICK on the **BOOKINGS.Holiday Number** field to place the insertion point and reverse the previous change : delete the **2** and TYPE **1** (because later examples in this guide use the original data).

6   Close the **Destinations** form window.

Customising a form

➤ **This task will show you how to customise an existing form.**

The easiest way to produce custom forms is to make a standard form using the FormWizard and then customise it using the Form Design window.

Parts of the Form Design window

The Form Design window has three sections. The Form Header is at the top. The Detail section, which contains the main parts of the form and is used to display the data from records, is in the middle. The Form Footer section appears at the bottom. These three sections can be re-sized; also, the size of a section can be reduced to zero, effectively eliminating it.

When the mouse pointer touches a place where a section can be re-sized, it changes shape to become a double-headed arrow passing through a black bar; these places, plus the edge of the form, are shown below.

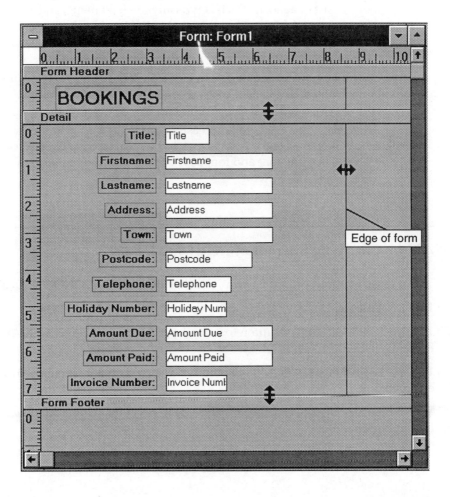

Selecting fields

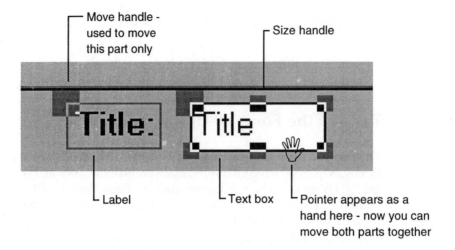

Move handle -
used to move
this part only

Size handle

Title:

Title

Label

Text box

Pointer appears as a
hand here - now you can
move both parts together

To select a single control, just click on it. Most controls represent a data field; they consist of a label, which is typically the field name, and a text box, where the data appears. You can select the label or the text box; both will then have a single move handle, but only the selected one will have the several small handles used for re-sizing the field.

The move handles enable you to move the label or the text box independently; to move both together, place the pointer on the edge of the selected field (it then appears as a hand) and drag both items to a new position.

After selecting a field, you can easily change the font, and the font size; you should then re-size the field to match the re-sized text. The two combo boxes, used to select the font and font size, appear near the center of the Toolbar only when a field is selected.

Activity 29.1 **Changing the font of fields and labels**

1   In the **Database** window, SELECT **Form** , SELECT **BOOKINGS**, CHOOSE **Design**.

2   SELECT the **Title** field.

3   SELECT the Font Indicator **list** button to view the available fonts, CHOOSE **Arial**. SELECT the Font Size **list** button, CHOOSE **12**.

4   SELECT the **Layout** menu, CHOOSE **Size to Fit**. The field area is increased in size to display the enlarged font.

5   DRAG the mouse pointer over all the other fields to select them; you can now change several fields with one operation.

6   SELECT the Font Indicator **list** button, CHOOSE **Arial**. SELECT the Font Size **list** button, CHOOSE **12**.

7   SELECT the **Layout** menu, CHOOSE **Size to Fit**. The **Form Design** window appears as follows.

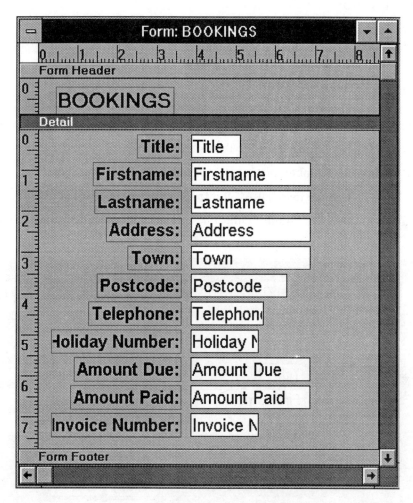

The fields appear as white rectangles; in Form view they will display data. Each field occupies whatever area is required to enable it to display data; if the field name is much longer than the data then only part of the field name will be visible when the form is in Design view.

8   SELECT the **File** menu, CHOOSE **Save**.

9   SELECT **Form View** button to view a record displayed in the new font.

The Size to Fit command does not always work perfectly. You may need to return to Design view and extend some fields, by dragging a Size handle to the right.

Activity 29.2 **Moving fields to a new position on a form**

1 In **Design** view, DRAG the edge of the **BOOKINGS** form to the right to increase the form width to 13 cm (5").

2 DRAG the mouse over the group of fields starting with **Address** and ending with **Postcode**; the fields become selected. DRAG this group of fields to the right and up, to position them to the right of **Title**, **Firstname** and **Address**.

3 SELECT the **Holiday Number** field.

4 Move the mouse pointer around over the **Holiday Number** field and field name; when the pointer is over the correct place for dragging this field to a new position, it appears as a hand.

5 DRAG the **Holiday Number** field to the right.

6 Repeat for **Invoice Number**, placing it underneath **Holiday Number**.

7 SELECT the **Telephone** field. DRAG it into the now empty position underneath **Lastname**.

8 SELECT and DRAG the **Amount Due** and **Amount Paid** fields to the right. The form design appears as follows.

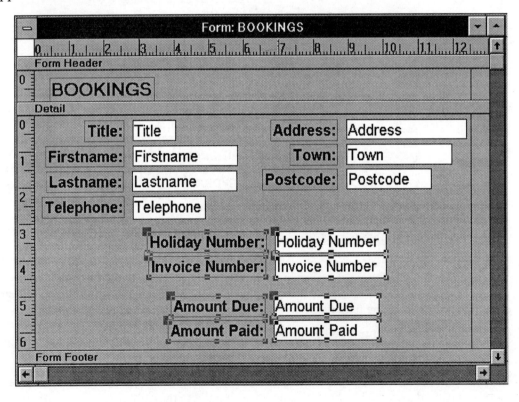

9 SELECT the **File** menu, CHOOSE **Save**.

10 SELECT the **Form View** button, to view the data.

```
┌─────────────────────────────────────────────────────────────┐
│ ⊟                    BOOKINGS                          ▼  ▲  │
├─────────────────────────────────────────────────────────────┤
│  BOOKINGS                                                    │
│ ▶  Title: [Mrs  ]        Address: [18 Cherry Grove]          │
│     Firstname: [Stella ]     Town: [Sleaford   ]            │
│     Lastname: [Wanda   ]  Postcode: [SL18 7TT ]            │
│     Telephone: [0529 7171]                                   │
│                                                              │
│              Holiday Number: [            2]                 │
│              Invoice Number: [            1]                 │
│                                                              │
│                  Amount Due: [     £999.00]                 │
│                 Amount Paid: [     £499.00]                 │
│                                                              │
│ ◄◄ ◄ Record:1  ► ►│                                          │
└─────────────────────────────────────────────────────────────┘
```

11 Close the form window.

➤ **This task will show you how to store a picture in a table, and then display the picture using a form.**

You can obtain images from various sources such as clip-art (which you buy), from a scanner which enables you to enter images from photographs etc into your computer, or by painting the image using a program such as Paintbrush. Here you will use Paintbrush, as this accessory is available to all Access users (because Paintbrush is included with Windows). Paintbrush can be used to paint company logos and other designs that you may wish to incorporate into a form or a report. For more information about Paintbrush, see your Microsoft Windows manual.

In an Access database, an OLE (Object Linking and Embedding) field is used to store pictures. You will add an OLE field to the Holidays table, and then use the Windows Clipboard to Paste in an example picture. You will then create a form to display the picture.

Activity 30.1   Using Paintbrush to paint a picture

1   Start Paintbrush and DRAG the mouse over the drawing area to paint a picture. I have painted an Angelfish, but you can produce a design of your own choosing. You will need to paint something for use in **Activity 30.2**, even if it is only a very simple picture.

2   SELECT the **Pick** tool (the right-hand **Scissors** button). Starting at the top left of your painting, DRAG the mouse down and to the right to enclose your picture in an outline. SELECT the **Edit** menu, CHOOSE **Copy** to copy your painting into the Clipboard.

3   Close the **Paintbrush** window.

Activity 30.2   Adding an OLE field to the HOLIDAYS table

1   Open Access. In the **Database** window, SELECT **Table**, SELECT **HOLIDAYS**, CHOOSE **Design**.

2   SELECT the **Field Name** field of the first blank row to place the insertion point. TYPE **Picture** and PRESS Tab to move the insertion point into the next field.

3   SELECT the **list** button, CHOOSE **OLE Object**. In the **Field Properties** section CLICK on the **Caption** field to place the insertion point, TYPE **Come and see...** Access will call this field Picture in the table design, but will give it the caption 'Come and see...' on a form.

4   SELECT the **File** menu, CHOOSE **Save**.

Activity 30.3 Pasting a Paintbrush picture into a record

1 SELECT **Datasheet** view; the table of holiday data appears.

2 CLICK on the **Picture** field for **Holiday Number 2**, to place the insertion point. SELECT the **Edit** menu, CHOOSE **Paste**; the words 'Paintbrush Picture' appear in the field.

3 Close the **Table** window.

4 In the **Database** window, SELECT **Form**, CHOOSE **New**. The **New Form** dialog appears.

5 SELECT the **list** button, CHOOSE **HOLIDAYS**. CHOOSE **FormWizards**.

6 CHOOSE **OK** (for a single column form), CLICK the '**>>**' button, CHOOSE **Next>**.

7 CHOOSE **Next>** to use the Standard look for your form, SELECT the **Design** button.

8 DRAG the edge of the form to the right, to increase the form width.

9 SELECT **Come and see...** in the field, then DRAG the field to the top right of the **Detail** section. DRAG the lower right corner handle up and to the left to reduce the field size.

10 DRAG the right-hand edge of the **Details** field to the right to enlarge it. The form design appears as follows.

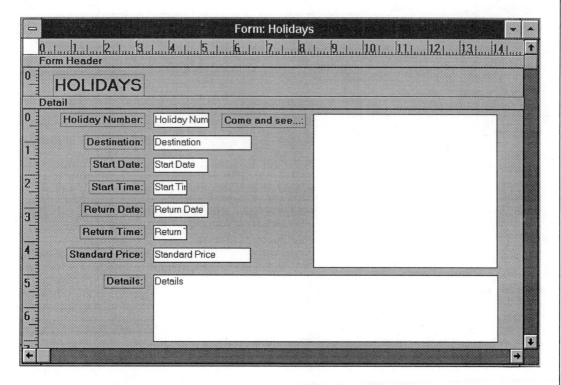

11 CHOOSE the **Form View** button. The form displays the data for **Holiday Number 1**. No picture has been entered into the **HOLIDAYS** table for this holiday.

12 CLICK the **Next Record** button; the record for **Holiday 2** appears. The **Come and see...** field displays the Paintbrush picture.

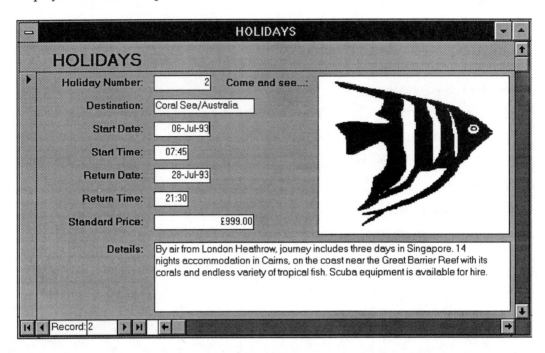

13 SELECT the **File** menu, CHOOSE **Save Form As**, TYPE **HOLIDAYS**, CHOOSE **OK**.

14 Close the form window.

Using charts and graphs

➤ **This task will show you how to create charts and graphs.**

Graphs and charts are widely used for the analysis of all kinds of numerical data, and they are a valuable presentation tool. Here you will use the GraphWizard to create a pie chart; other types of chart and graph can be produced in the same way. This task uses the query saved as Bookings by Destination in Activity 20.2.

Activity 31.1 **Creating a pie chart of bookings by destination**

1 SELECT the **Form** button in the **Database** window, CHOOSE **New**. The **New Form** dialog appears. SELECT the **list** button, CHOOSE **Bookings by Destination**.

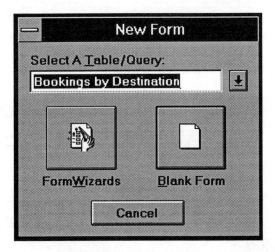

2 SELECT **FormWizards**. A new dialog appears.

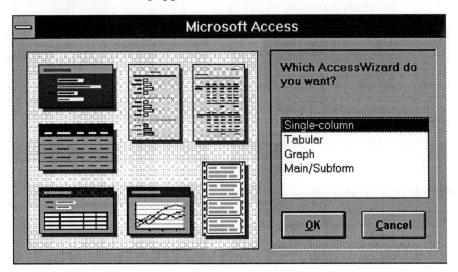

3   CHOOSE **Graph**, CHOOSE **OK**. The **GraphWizard** dialog appears.

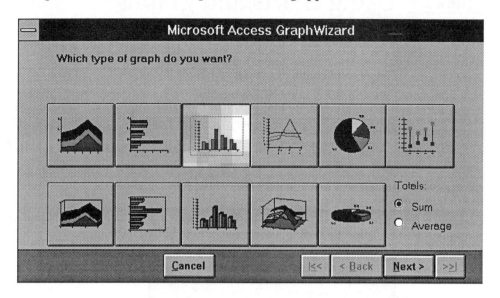

4   SELECT the **Pie Chart** button, SELECT **Next>**. A new **GraphWizard** dialog appears.

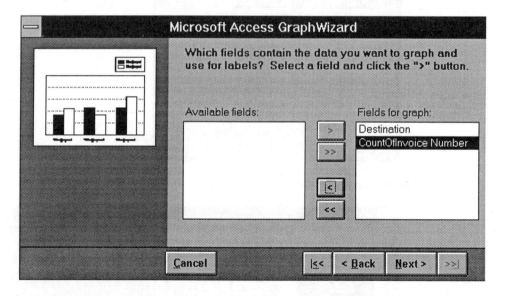

5   SELECT the '**>>**' button to move all the fields into the **Fields for graph** box.

6   SELECT **Next>**. A new **GraphWizard** dialog appears.

7   TYPE **Pie of Bookings by Destination** as the graph title.

8   CHOOSE the **Open** button; a four-colour pie chart appears.

9   SELECT the **File** menu, CHOOSE **Save Form As**.

10 TYPE **Pie of Bookings by Destination**. SELECT **OK**, CHOOSE **Yes**.

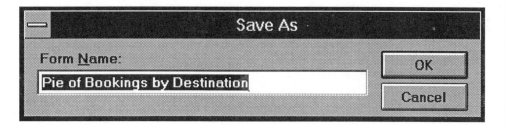

The Form displaying your pie chart adopts the new name. The form name does not have to be the same as the form title, although if they are the same this makes it easier to remember what it does. Any brief descriptive name is OK.

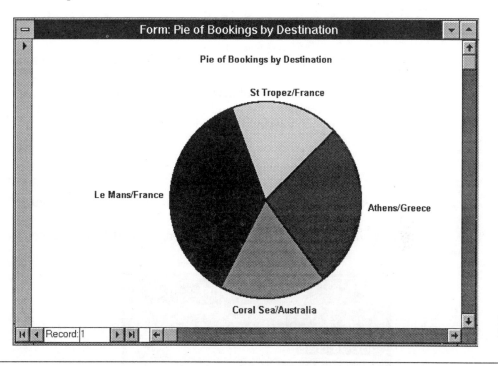

Activity 31.2 **Printing the chart**

1 SELECT the **File** menu, CHOOSE **Print**. The **Print** dialog appears.

2 CHOOSE **OK**. Only the chart is printed - the scroll bars etc do not appear. On a black and white printer, the colours will be replaced by shades of grey.

3 Close the **Form** window.

Section F
Producing reports

Task 32: To create, use and print a report

Task 33: To customise a report

Task 32 Creating and printing a report

➤ **This task will show you how to create and print a simple report.**

A report is a printed list of data which may include totals, counts and other summary information; although you can print your data directly from tables, reports give you greater control over how the data is presented.

Activity 32.1   **Creating a report showing all the current bookings**

1   In the **Database** window SELECT the **Report** button, SELECT **New**; the **New Report** dialog appears.

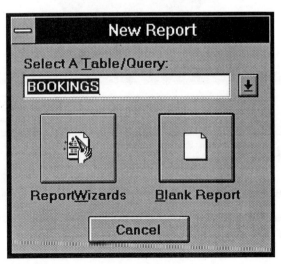

2   SELECT the **list** button, CHOOSE **BOOKINGS**.

3   CHOOSE **ReportWizards**.

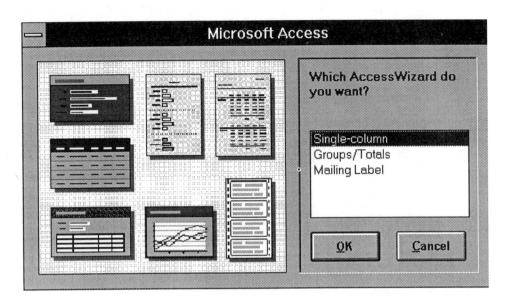

4   CHOOSE **OK** to use the (already selected) **Single-column** option; the **ReportWizard** dialog appears.

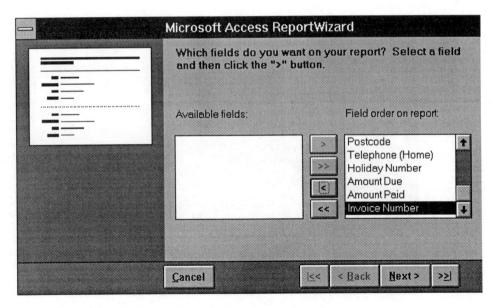

5   SELECT the '>>' button to move the field names from the **Available fields** section into the **Field order on report** section. SELECT **Next>**.

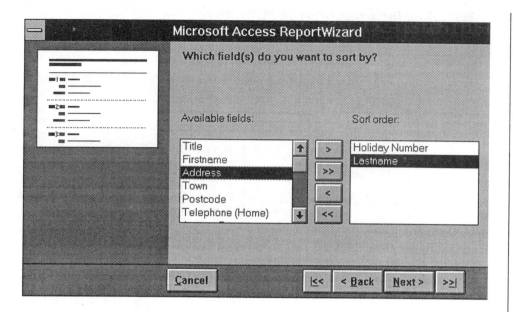

6   SELECT **Holiday Number** in the **Available fields** section, CLICK the '>' button to move this field name into the **Sort order** section.

7   SELECT **Lastname** and CLICK the '>' button.

8   SELECT **Next>**.

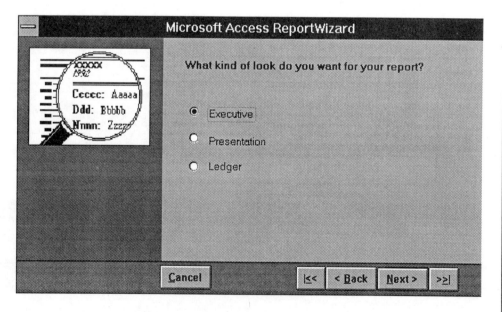

9   SELECT **Next>** to accept the default 'Executive' look for your report.

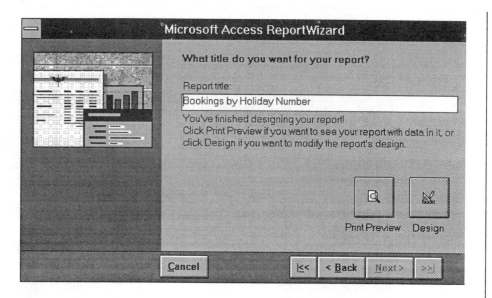

10 TYPE **Bookings by Holiday Number** to replace the default title.

11 CHOOSE **Print Preview** to see how the report will appear.

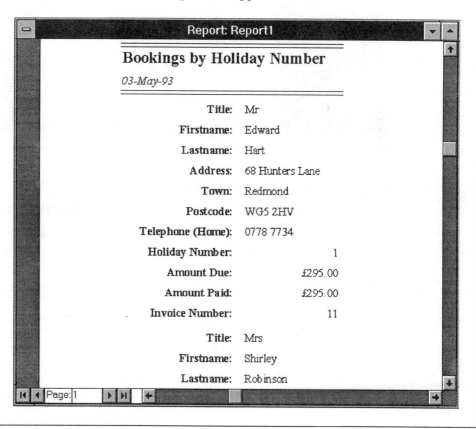

Activity 32.2   Using Zoom to view a report

1   CLICK anywhere on the report to 'zoom out' so that you can view the page layout.

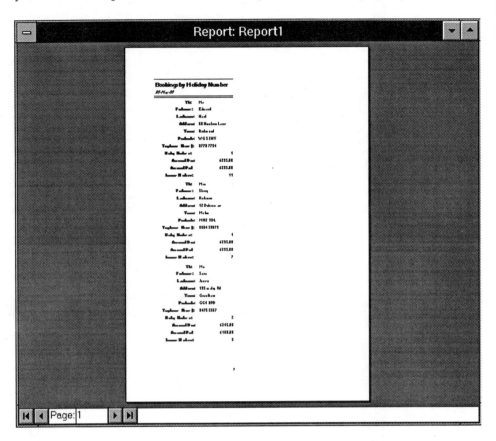

2   CLICK on the report again to 'zoom in' so that you can view the details.

You can also use the navigation buttons at each side of the Page Number indicator to view the next/previous or first/last pages.

Activity 32.3   Printing a report

1   From the **Print Preview** window, SELECT the **Print** button.
2   SELECT **OK** to start printing.

Activity 32.4   Saving a report

1   If you are in *Print Preview mode*, CHOOSE the **Cancel** button to exit.

2   SELECT the **File** menu, CHOOSE **Save As**, TYPE **Bookings by Holiday Number**, CLICK **OK**.

After you save your report design, you can re-use it as required to generate an up-to-date copy of the report. The report name does not have to be the same as the report title, although if it is the same then this makes it easier to remember what it does. The rules for report names are the same as those for naming fields, tables etc as described in Task 2.

Activity 32.5   Closing a report

1   DOUBLE-CLICK on the report **Control-menu** box to close the report and return to the **Database** window.

Activity 32.6   Opening a report

1   From the **Database** window SELECT **Report**, SELECT **Bookings by Holiday Number**.

2   CHOOSE the **Preview** button. The report design is re-run to produce a new report; if the data in the database has changed, then the new report will reflect this.

3   Close the report.

Activity 32.7   Deleting a report

1   In the **Database** window SELECT the **Report** button.

2   SELECT **Bookings by Holiday Number**.

3   SELECT the **Edit** menu, CHOOSE **Delete**.

4   CHOOSE **OK** to confirm the deletion.

Customising a report

➤ **This task will show you how to customise a standard report made using the ReportWizard.**

Parts of the Report Design window

The Report Design window has a Report Header and a Page Header section at the top, followed by the main Detail section. At the bottom are the Page Footer and Report Footer sections. These sections can be re-sized; and the size can be reduced to zero, effectively eliminating a section (as in the Page Header, below). When the mouse pointer touches a place where a section can be re-sized, it changes shape to become a double-headed arrow passing through a black bar; these places are indicated on the following illustration.

How much of the Report window you can view will depend upon whether you are using Standard-VGA or Super-VGA.

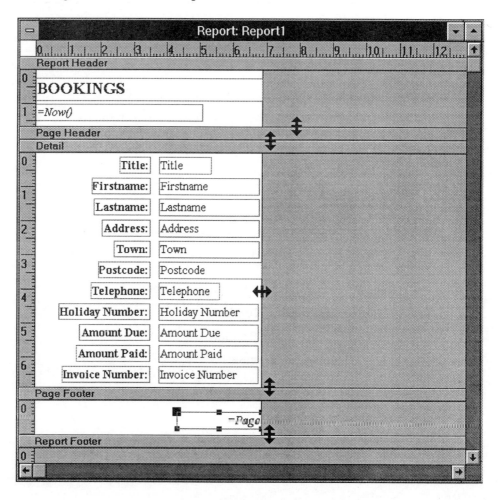

Changing the Report Design

The design view of a report looks much like the design view of a form, and is edited in the same way.

The text and data that appear on the printed report are represented by **controls** in Design view. For example, the design of the single-column report created in Activity 32.1 will contain controls to print the report header, today's date, lines and fields from the bookings table.

When you select a control that represents text, the Toolbar will display buttons for selecting font, font size, attributes (bold, italic, underline), and alignment of the text. There are two types of control, each of these having several varieties.

A **bound control** shows data taken from a table (possibly via a query). When the report is run Access 'binds' the data from the table to these controls. To add a bound control to your report, drag a field name from the field list and position it where you want the data to appear on the report.

An **unbound control** represents static items such as labels, lines and rectangles, or a calculated result. None of these directly uses data from a table, so Access does not have to 'bind' data to them when the report is run (the calculation uses data which, by this time, is already in the report). To add an unbound control, drag a control from the Toolbox and place it on the report at the position where you wish the item to appear. To add a calculated control, drag the Text Box tool onto the report and type in a formula starting with an equals ('=') sign.

Date and Time

Each PC contains an electronic clock that maintains the date and time. The appeerence of the function **=Now()** in a report causes the current date and time to be added to the report when it is produced.

Page Layout

Because reports are intended for printing, you need to consider the page layout.

To change the page layout in Report Design view, select File and then choose Print Setup (or select the Print Setup button in Print Preview). There are options for changing settings that are specific to your printer. You can choose a particular paper size and a particular paper tray (if more than one is available).

By default the report will be printed on the default printer (as set in Windows). If you have more than one printer, then the default setting may be changed (perhaps by someone else) and it is better to select the Specific Printer button and choose a particular printer from the list of those installed via Windows.

Instead of the usual 'Portrait' (vertical) orientation, you can choose 'Landscape' to print sideways across the page (the paper will still pass through your printer in the usual way).

A report to print invoices

Here you will produce a custom report to print invoices for those clients who have not yet fully paid for their package holiday.

The records will be selected from the BOOKINGS and HOLIDAYS tables using the query previously saved as Outstanding Balances in Activity 19.1. This provides an easy way to add fields from more than one table.

When the report is run, the query is automatically run. The query will ask for a Holiday Number to be entered, and then will select all records for this holiday where the balance is greater than zero. The report will take this dynaset and print an invoice for each record.

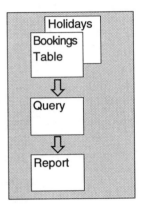

This is a good example of a task that needs a long list of instructions, but which, after a little practice, can be done very quickly!

The fonts referred to below are included with Windows 3.1.

Activity 33.1 **Creating a custom report to print invoices**

1 From the **Database** window SELECT **Report**, CHOOSE **New**.

2 SELECT the **list** button in the **New Report** dialog, CHOOSE **Outstanding Balances**.

3 CHOOSE **ReportWizards**.

4 CLICK on **OK** to choose the (already selected) **Single Column** option.

5 SELECT **Invoice Number** in the **Available fields** box, CLICK the '>' button; SELECT **BALANCE**, CLICK the '>' button.

6 CLICK the '>>' button to add all the other fields.

7 CHOOSE **Next>** to display a new dialog.

8 SELECT **Lastname**, CHOOSE '>', SELECT **Firstname**, CHOOSE '>'. CHOOSE **Next>**.

9 CHOOSE **Next>** to use the default 'Executive' look.

10 CHOOSE **Design**; the **Report** design window appears.

11 DRAG the right-hand border of the page to the right, to give a page width of about 6" (15cm).

12 DRAG the horizontal bar labelled **Detail** down by about 2/3" (1.5cm). The mouse pointer changes shape when it is positioned correctly for this operation.

13 SELECT the **=Now()** field and DRAG it down and to the right, into the **Details** section, placing it to the right of the **Invoice Number** field.

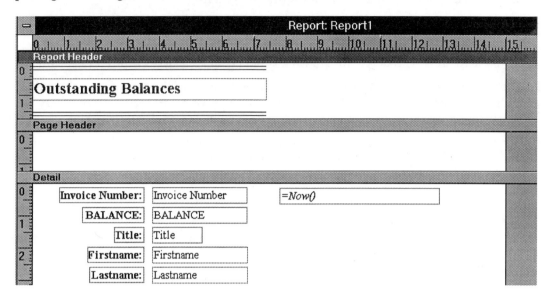

14 SELECT the field containing the text **Outstanding Balances**; wait a short time (so as not to double-click), then CLICK on the **Print Invoices** field again to place the insertion point.

15 PRESS Backspace to delete the existing text, TYPE **Sunshine Holidays**.

16 CLICK on the right-hand edge of this field to select it and DRAG the field down, to the center of the **Page Header** section.

17 SELECT the Font Indicator **list** button on the Toolbar, CHOOSE **Times New Roman**.

18 SELECT the Font Size **list** button, CHOOSE a point size of **28**, SELECT **Center Paragraph**.

19 SELECT the **Layout** menu, CHOOSE **Size to Fit**.

20 The original report heading had two lines above it and two lines below it; SELECT each line in turn and PRESS Del to delete it.

21 DRAG the horizontal bar labelled **Page Header** up to reduce the size of the **Report Header** section to zero.

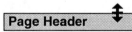

22 If necessary, use the vertical scroll-bar to view the last fields in the **Detail** section.

23 DRAG the mouse over the group of fields starting at the top left of **Holiday Number** and ending at the bottom right of **Return Date**; when you release the mouse button the fields become selected. DRAG these fields to the right and up, so that **Holiday Number** is approximately to the right of the **Firstname** field.

24 DRAG the **Title, Firstname, Lastname, Address, Town,** and **Postcode** fields down a little to horizontally line up **Title** and **Holiday Number**.

25 If necessary, SELECT the **View** menu, CHOOSE **Toolbox**; the **Toolbox** appears.

26 SELECT the **Label** button in the **Toolbox** (the 'A' button).

27 CHOOSE the **Align Paragraph Left** button on the Toolbar.

28 Move the mouse pointer onto the **Detail** section, to the left, below the fields, and DRAG the mouse to the right and down, to create a text field about 5" (12cm) wide and 1" (2cm) tall.

29 TYPE the following text: **Please forward to us the balance of the cost of your Sunshine Holiday, as shown above. We can accept all well-known credit cards, alternatively we will be pleased to accept your cheque by post or cash from personal callers.**

30 Use the scroll-bar to view the **Page Footer** section of the report; SELECT the **=Page** field, PRESS Del to delete it (on a multipage report, this field would hold the page number, but on our single page invoices we do not need it).

31 Place the mouse pointer in the **Details** section (but not on a field) and DOUBLE-CLICK to display the **Section** dialog which lists the properties for this section.

32 SELECT Force New Page **list** button, CHOOSE **After Section** (this will cause each invoice to begin on a new page).

33 Close the **Section** dialog window. The report design appears as follows.

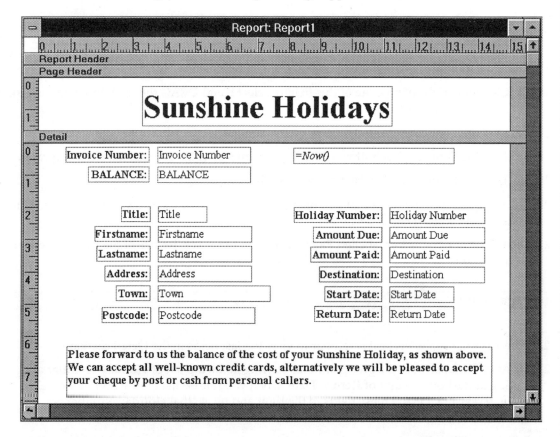

34 SELECT the **File** menu, CHOOSE **Save As**, TYPE **Print Invoices**, CHOOSE **OK**.

35 SELECT the **Print Preview** button; the **Enter Parameter Value** dialog appears.

36 TYPE **3** and SELECT **OK**.

37 CHOOSE **Print** to print the series of invoices for **Holiday Number 3**. The first invoice will display the following information.

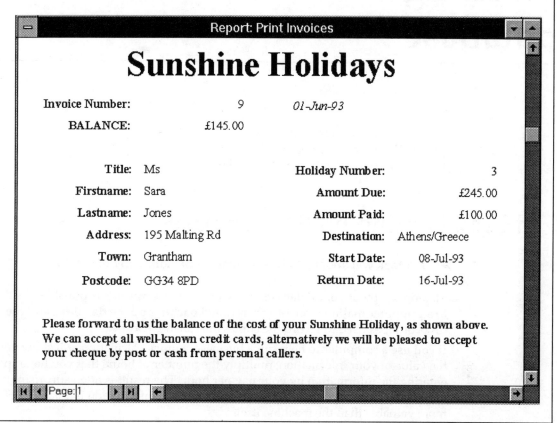

Section G
Working with the whole database

Task 34: To back up the database
Task 35: To rename or delete a database
Task 36: To permanently link two tables

| Task 34 | Backing up the database

> ➤ **This task will show you how to make a backup copy of a database.**

Making a copy of your database file as an insurance against its possible loss due to a computer malfunction, fire etc is called **backing up** the database, and the disks or tapes used to record the copies are called **backups**.

If you use a computer to help run a business, a quick calculation will show you the value of your information; multiply the number of hours that you have spent entering the information by your pay per hour. The result is often surprising; after using the computer for quite a short time, the information it holds is often more valuable than the machine itself.

Information recorded once (example, on your hard disk) is never 100% safe, and you should always copy the information to another medium - usually a floppy disk or tape - at the end of each session in which information has been changed.

An Access database is stored on disk as a single file which contains all the components of the database - tables, forms, stored queries, reports etc - together with the data that has been entered. This simplifies backing up the database.

Activity 34.1 **Making a copy of sunhols.mdb called test.mdb.**

1   Open the **File Manager** (in the Windows **Program Manager** window).

2   SELECT **Access** in the **Directory Tree** section (to the left), SELECT **sunhols.mdb** in the **Files** section (to the right). SELECT the **File** menu, CHOOSE **Copy**.

3   TYPE **TEST.MDB** then CHOOSE **OK**. Close the **File Manager** window.

Task 35 | Renaming or deleting a database

> ➤ **This task will show you how to rename an existing database, or delete one that is no longer required.**

To rename a database, use the Windows File Manager to rename the .MDB file. The new name must be a DOS filename; briefly, the new name can be up to eight characters long, and must not contain any spaces. The name is not case sensitive.

When you start Access and select the File menu, the original database name may still appear in the list that appears at the foot of the File menu; but when you select the Open Database option, only the new name will appear in the list of databases.

Activity 35.1   **Renaming test.mdb to be called testbase.mdb**

1   Open the **File Manager** (in the Windows **Program Manager** window).

2   SELECT **Access** in the **Directory Tree** section (to the left), SELECT **test.mdb** in the **Files** section (right).

3   SELECT the **File** menu, CHOOSE **Rename.**

4   TYPE **testbase.mdb** and then CHOOSE **OK**.

5   Close the **File Manager** window.

Deleting a database

To delete a database, use the Windows File Manager to delete the .MDB file.

The name of the deleted database may still appear in the list of recently used database names that appears at the foot of the File menu. As you use other databases, the unwanted name will eventually be displaced.

Activity 35.2   **Deleting testbase.mdb**

1   In **File Manager** SELECT **Access**, SELECT **testbase.mdb.**

2   SELECT the **File** menu, CHOOSE **Delete.**

3   CLICK **OK**, CHOOSE **Yes** to confirm that you wish to delete this file. Close the **File Manager** window.

Task 36 Permanently linking tables

➤ **This task will show you how to establish a permanent relationship between two tables.**

When performing queries using data from both the BOOKINGS and HOLIDAYS tables, you have forged a link between them using the data in the Holidays Number fields. Here you will permanently link Holiday Number in the HOLIDAYS table with Holiday Number in the BOOKINGS table.

The two fields to be linked could have different names, but must contain related data - the data are used to make the connection, not the field names. The two fields must be of the same data type; except that a Long Integer field can be linked to a Counter field.

You can define only one relationship between two tables; if you define a second relationship, it replaces the first one. If you wish to delete a table, you must delete a table's relationships first.

Primary key and Primary table

The field from at least one table must be a primary key; this ensures that there cannot be any duplicate entries (if both fields contain duplicate entries, Access cannot link them in any useful way). The Holiday Number field in the HOLIDAYS table is a primary key.

In a 'One-to-Many' relationship (example, one Holiday may have many people booked to go on it) the table with the one (Holiday) is the Primary Table and the table with the many (Bookings) is the related table.

Referential Integrity

The Relationships dialog has a check box labelled Referential Integrity. This sounds complicated, but it is an option that is 'common sense' once you understand what it does. Selecting this option tells Access to:

1 Prevent you from entering a Holiday Number in the BOOKINGS table, when a holiday of that number does not exist in the HOLIDAYS table. It does not make sense to enter bookings for a holiday which does not exist, or about which you have no information.

2 Prevent you from deleting a holiday record from the HOLIDAYS table if there are clients booked to go on that holiday. If you were to delete a record from the HOLIDAYS table, whilst there were still clients booked to go on that tour, these clients would be left booked onto a holiday about which there was no information available.

Activity 36.1   Permanently linking HOLIDAYS and BOOKINGS

1   In the **Database** window, SELECT **Table**, CLICK once on **HOLIDAYS** to highlight the table name.

2   SELECT the **Edit** menu, CHOOSE **Relationships**. The **Relationships** window appears, with **HOLIDAYS** already selected in the **Primary Table** list box.

3   SELECT the Related Table **list** button, SELECT **BOOKINGS**.

4   Optionally, SELECT the **Referential Integrity** check box.

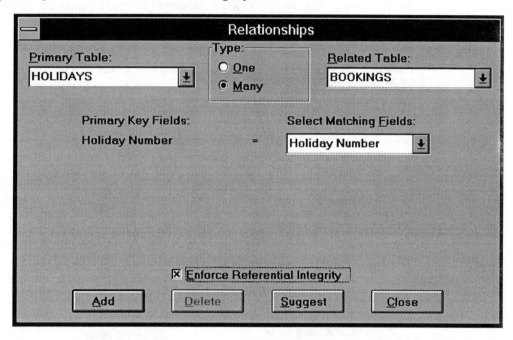

5   CHOOSE **Add**, CHOOSE **Close**.

Now there will be no need to link the two tables each time you design queries that use data from these tables. The link will appear by default.

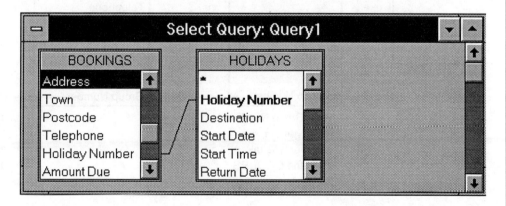

Appendix A: Adding tables to the database

A database can have almost any number of tables; the maximum is 32768 - a greater number than even a large company is actually likely to need! Many databases have only one or two tables, but a database for business use will often have more. Once you have discovered how to create and use a database with two tables, then adding additional tables is easy. By way of example, if you were to add another table to the SUNHOLS database to store the extra information required when bookings are made by schools, social clubs etc, you would perform the following two steps:-

Firstly... Create a new table (called, for example, GROUPS) to hold the additional information. Make one field a primary key so that no duplicate data items are allowed in that field; a Counter field is a good choice for this purpose.

Secondly... Add a corresponding field to one of the original tables, so that the two can be linked; the linking fields must have the same data type (except that a Long Integer number can be linked to a Counter field).

In the illustration below the Group Number field in the new GROUPS table is a Counter field; the Group Number field in the BOOKINGS table is a Long Integer number. When data is entered for a new group booking, the new group is first entered into the GROUPS table, where the Group Number is generated automatically. This Group Number is then entered into the BOOKINGS table together with the data for each individual who is booked as part of the group.

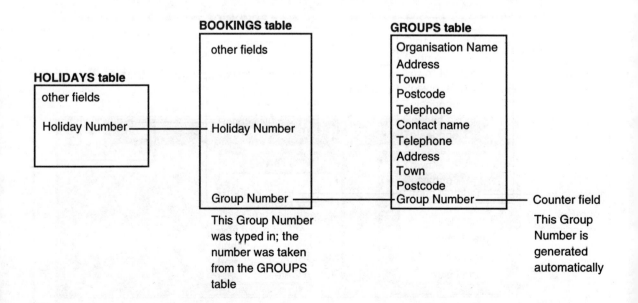

Appendix B: Some Toolbar buttons

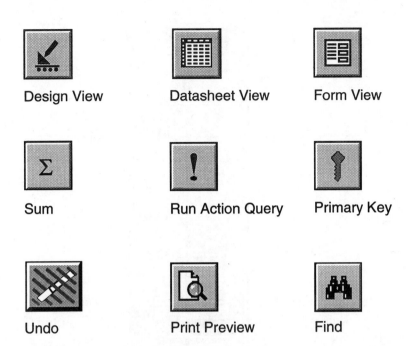

Design View

Datasheet View

Form View

Sum

Run Action Query

Primary Key

Undo

Print Preview

Find

The following will appear only when a label or field is selected:

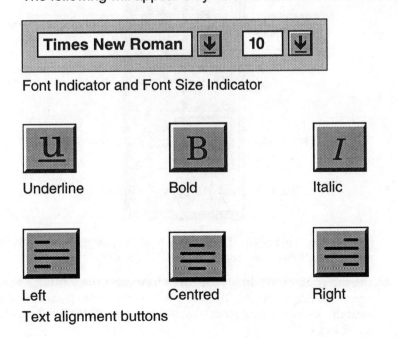

Font Indicator and Font Size Indicator

Underline

Bold

Italic

Left

Centred

Right

Text alignment buttons

Appendix C: Toolbox buttons

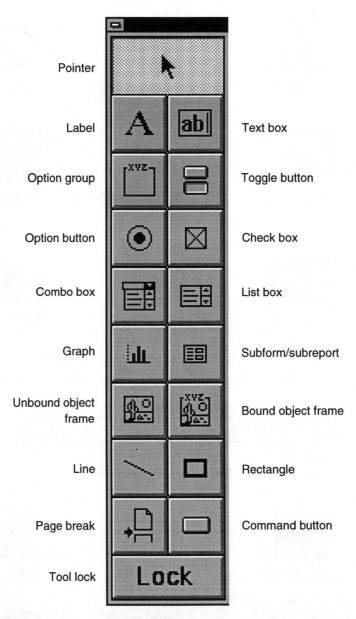

Pointer

Label

Text box

Option group

Toggle button

Option button

Check box

Combo box

List box

Graph

Subform/subreport

Unbound object frame

Bound object frame

Line

Rectangle

Page break

Command button

Tool lock

If the Toolbox is not displayed when you are using form or report design view, then SELECT the View menu, CHOOSE Toolbox.

Use the Toolbox to add objects – which Access calls controls – to a form or report. To add a control, SELECT the tool, move the pointer to the desired location on the form or report (in design view), then CLICK or DRAG to place the object.

Appendix D: Functions and operators

Functions

Sum	Total of the values within a field
Avg	Average of the values within a field
Min	Lowest value within a field
Max	Highest value within a field
Count	Number of values within a field (excluding null values)
StDev	Standard deviation of the values within a field
Var	Variance of values within a field
First	First value within a field
Last	Last value within a field
=Now	Current date (used on forms and in reports)

Operators

+	Addition
-	Subtraction
*	Multiplication
/	Division
\	Integer division (integer part of the result of dividing one integer by another)
Mod	Modulus (remainder of dividing one integer by another)

Comparison operators

=	Equal to
<>	Not equal to
>	Greater than
>=	Greater than or equal to
<	Less than
<=	Less than or equal to
Between *value1* and *value2*	Between two values (inclusive)
In *value1, value2, value3* etc	Occurs in the list of values given
Is Null	Has no value
Like *pattern*	Matches a pattern (that can include wildcards)

Glossary

Access A software program used to build databases.

Action query A type of query that updates or deletes some of the data stored in the database. Only records that fit the selection criteria are changed.

And A keyword used in queries where the data to be selected has to meet more than one criterion. For example, you may wish to view the data for those people who are booked for Holiday Number 2 *and* live in Boston.

Application A piece of software that performs some task directly useful to the user. Strictly speaking, Access is not an application, because you cannot do anything useful with Access without first building a database application. In this sense, Access is a development tool, used to produce a software application. By comparison, a word processor is an application because you can begin typing letters etc straight away.

Asterisk In Access, a wildcard used to represent any number of characters. For example, M* represents all words beginning with the letter M.

Base table A standard database term. A base table is used to hold the data that you have entered into the database; everything else derives its data from these base tables.

Bound control A control is an element that appears on a form or a report. A bound control is used to enter, or display, data stored in a table.

Byte A unit of information in the computer memory or on a disk. One character occupies one byte; simple graphics can be stored using a few bytes, whilst complex graphics may need much more.

Calculated field A field in a table, form or report used to display the result of a calculation performed upon data taken from other fields.

Click When you place the mouse pointer on a screen object (for example, a button or a menu option) and press the left-hand mouse button to select or activate that object, you are said to click the mouse.

Close When you have finished using a window containing a form, table etc, you can close the window to remove it from your screen. One way of closing a window is to double-click on its Control-menu box.

Control-menu A small box that appears at the top left-hand corner of a window, displaying a 'Spacebar' symbol. You can click on this box to display a menu (not often used) or double-click to close the window.

Control	In Access, any object on a form or report.
Counter	A special data type that may be used in a table. A counter is a number (Long Integer) that automatically increments by one each time a new record is added. It may be used to generate a unique number for each record, often used for such things as an Invoice Number.
Cue card	A part of the help system that shows you the basic operations needed to produce tables. Users who have received some training will probably not use Cue cards.
Data	A piece of information without the context that gives it meaning. In a database, the context is entered once when a table is designed, as a field name (column heading) perhaps with a comment; the table itself contains data.
Database	An organised collection of facts. A computerised database created using Access will store information in tables, and enable you to manage this information using forms, queries and reports.
Data entry	The task of entering data; this can be a specialised job if the database is to contain a great amount of information.
Datasheet view	A display of a table, query, form or report when it is being used to show data in tabular form (as opposed to Design view).
Data type	A definition that governs what kind of data you can enter into a field.
DBMS	DataBase Management System. As well as storing your information, a DBMS such as Access enables you to manage your information more efficiently than by using manual methods.
Default	A pre-set value; for example, number fields default to zero.
Design view	A display of a table, query, form or report that will enable you to view or edit the design.
Dialog box	A window that enables you to type in some additional information needed by Access to perform a command, or to select options.
Double-click	The action of placing the pointer on a screen item and then tapping the left-hand button twice (quickly!).

Drag The action of moving the mouse whilst continuously pressing the left-hand mouse button. This may be used to select a piece of text, or to select, move or re-size objects on a form or report (in Design view).

Dynaset The 'answer table' that is produced when you run a query. It differs from a base table in that it is a temporary thing (a new one is created each time you run the query) and it may contain data taken from more than one table. The data in a dynaset can be used with forms, reports and graphs.

Field A space for a specified piece of data; the vertical columns of a table are made up of fields.

Foreign key A field, other than a primary key field, that may be used to link tables together.

Form An on-screen version of a fill-in-the-blank printed form, used for entering or viewing the information in a table.

Form view A display of a form when it is being used to show data, as opposed to Design view.

FormWizard A software component in Access that asks you to select various options needed to create a standard type of form and then creates the form for you.

Function A built-in formula used in calculations. A function consists of a function name followed by a pair of parentheses; these usually contain the name(s) of the field(s) that the calculation is to be performed upon. Functions operate on all the fields in a column of a table, or sub-groups of these.

Index Optionally, the fields in a table may be indexed. An index file contains information about the location of records in a table so as to enable records to be located quickly, using the value in the indexed fields. The entry and updating of data are slowed because, when the new data is saved, the indexes must be updated and saved too. Indexes are most beneficial when used with a large database (many records) and where the data is frequently retrieved but not often updated.

Insertion point A small flashing vertical bar that is used with text or numbers to show you where 'you are at'. Anything that you type will appear at the position of the insertion point. The British often call it a cursor.

Integer A whole number; one with no decimal places.

Keyword	A word that Access 'understands'. Access understands only a few words.
Label	A piece of text on a form or report used to enhance appearance or give context to the data displayed.
Memo	A special field that may appear in a table or on a form. Used to hold text where the length of some entries may be quite long (up to 32,000 characters). Technically, the memo is not part of a table - the table contains a pointer to the memo, which is stored elsewhere. Because of this you can perform only a few kinds of operation on a memo field.
Null value	A field that has had no data entered, and which does not automatically adopt a default value, is said to contain a null value. A null value signifies that the data is unknown or inapplicable.
Object	A component of the database, such as a table, form, query or report; or a component of one of these objects, such as a field in a table, any item on a form or report including lines and rectangles used to enhance appearance. An object has an independent existence - it can be moved or copied, for example.
One-to-many	Two tables may have a one-to-many relationship, where each row in one table can be linked to many rows in the other. For example, HOLIDAYS has a one-to-many relationship with BOOKINGS.
Open	To display the contents of an object such as a table or form in a window. When you open a stored query, the query is run and the results are displayed.
Operator	A symbol that represents an action to be performed in a calculation.
Or	An Access keyword used in queries to link two parts of a selection criterion together when you wish for the record to be selected when either criterion is true. For example, the criteria for selecting some records may be that the client lives in Boston *or* Seaton.
Paintbrush	A software application, included with Windows, that enables you to paint and edit pictures made up from pixels (small dots).
Parameter	Used in a query, a parameter is a substitute for an item of data that will be entered later, when the query is run. This enables you to re-use a query many times, but select different records each time by entering a different parameter when the query is run.

Primary key	A field in a table which has been specified as a primary key. The data entered into each field must be unique, so enabling it to be used to identify one particular record. Social security numbers, employee numbers, invoice numbers etc generated by a Counter field are often used as a primary key field.
Primary table	When two tables are linked using a one-to-many relationship, then the 'one' side of the link is said to be the primary table; the related field in this table must be a primary key.
QBE	Query-by-Example. A simple but sophisticated method of retrieving particular information from the database. The query is specified by filling in parts of a special table, called a QBE grid.
Query	A means of asking questions about your data, or of looking up specific information, or of isolating groups of records. The information is displayed in a type of table called a dynaset; a new dynaset is produced each time the query is run, so that if the data in the database has been changed, then this is reflected in the new dynaset. A query may be saved as a stored query and re-used any number of times. Queries can select records using more complex criteria than can be used with the Find command, and can be used to perform calculations.
Record	Another name for the data in one row of a table. Before computerised databases were used, each record would be written onto a card and stored in a card box.
Relational database	A database in which the data is stored in tables that are structured so that unnecessary duplication of data is avoided. The separate tables may be related (linked) by using the data in two related fields, one from each table.
Report	A printed document listing data from one table or dynaset. A report may include summary information such as totals and averages.
ReportWizard	A software component in Access that asks you to select various options needed to create a standard type of report and then creates the report for you.
Select	(1) To mark an item on-screen so that a subsequent action can be performed on that item. You usually select an item by clicking on it with the mouse, or dragging the mouse over the item. (2) To choose certain records from a table because they match particular criteria.
Status bar	A line at the bottom of the Access window displaying a piece of information that is useful in the current context. For example, when using a menu, a brief description of the currently selected option appears on the status bar.
Sum	The total produced by adding a set of numbers.

System date/time Each PC contains an electronic clock that maintains the system date and time; this enables Access to obtain the date and time from the computer system for use in reports etc.

Table A table contains information about one particular aspect of the business, such as customers, products, or orders, arranged neatly into rows (records) and columns (fields).

Text box Used in a dialog box; it is a box into which you type some additional information needed by Access to carry out a command.

Title bar The horizontal bar at the top of a window that displays the name of the window. Often, the title bar also contains the Control-menu box and the Maximise and Minimise buttons.

Toolbar Located near the top of the screen, the toolbar contains various buttons that you can use as a short-cut to choosing an option from a menu.

Toolbox A small window that may be used when customising forms and reports; it enables new items to be added to the design. The Toolbox is visible on your screen when the Toolbox option in the View menu is selected.

Unbound control An object in a form or report, such as a line, rectangle, or piece of text, that does not hold a piece of data taken from a table.

Undo In the Edit menu there is an Undo command that **in some circumstances** will enable you to reverse the previous operation.

Value The value of a field is the data item that it contains. For example, a Lastname field for one client may have 'Jones' entered into it; 'Jones' is its value. See also Null value.

Wildcard A character that represents one or more other characters. The asterisk is the most useful wildcard character; it is used to represent any character or group of characters. For example, M* represents any word that begins with the letter 'M'.

Window A rectangular area on your screen that is used to display a table, document, dialog box etc to the user.

Zoom The degree of enlargement of a form, report or similar screen object when viewed on your screen. When you 'zoom in', a small area of the screen is expanded so that you can view the details. When you 'zoom out', the details are reduced in size so that you can view more of the whole.

Index